"It's rare when a man has the courage to share his personal struggle with sexual addiction. It's unheard of to have his wife write the story with complete openness and love. Janet and Bruce Wheeler dispel the myths as they share their story, which is one of struggle, brokenness, and redemption. *Now Choose Life!* is a must read for those who struggle with sexual addiction and those whose lives sexual addiction has affected."

—**Kip McCormick**, Pastor & Executive Director,
Courageous Warrior Ministries

"*Now Choose Life!* is a wonderful resource that will inform, inspire, motivate and remind every couple that there is hope ahead! Bruce shares raw details of his life journey out of the grip of sexual addiction. His story is inspiring, illustrating that there is hope for the sex addict even after divorce. Janet shares her insights about sex addiction and how devastating the behaviors are to addicts and those who love them. This book will help addicts, partners, families and the friends who love them."

—**Cory M. Schortzman**,
Executive Director at Transformed Hearts
Counseling Center in Colorado Springs, Colorado

"For the thousands of people struggling with sexual addiction and all the people close to them, Janet Wheeler has written a powerful book that will help bring true freedom. She courageously kicks open the door, pulls back the covers and exposes the raw truth about the habits related to sexual obsession. Then she steps back and gracefully explains the journey from a secret life to a pure heart. For my coaching ministry I will keep a stock of *Now Choose Life!* on hand as lethal ammunition in the battle against the darkness."

—**Rev. E.S. Toby Quirk**,
Retired Army Officer, Pastor and Life Coach

"As a former pornography connoisseur and now a counselor helping men overcome pornography and couples, affairs, I find *Now Choose Life!* a much needed resource for those addicted to pornography and those who love them. It will help them find hope, understanding, and healing both as individuals and as a couple, by developing a "we" mentality as they face the compulsive sexual behavior, fears, feelings, and the recovery process. Bruce's experiences provide credibility to those addicted and help encourage them to face and seek the source of their own addiction. Without condoning the behavior, *Now Choose Life!* exudes a sensitivity and grace, motivated by Christ's love, to the addict, nurturing them in a way that a healthy sexual life can eventually be experienced. Easily, the most comprehensive book on this subject for both the faith-based and secular communities."

—Dr. Clarence Shuler, President/CEO,
BLR: Building Lasting Relationships Center

"I believe this is a great resource for both men and women who struggle with this growing issue in their lives. It is the root cause of many divorces and is a growing trend in our marriages, society and nation. People are looking for answers. Until people can break loose from the grip of their own past, pain, sin and addiction they will never reach their God-given potential and destiny. *Now Choose Life!* provides many of the answers we all need."

—Dr. Dan and Cathy Erickson,
Authors of *God Loves Do Overs!*

"*Now Choose Life!* is an insightful book that delves into a "forbidden" subject—sexual addiction and pornography. The damage they cause both the addict and those close to them is very real and painful. This book, written from the hearts of two courageous Christians, with God's guidance and love, will provide a deep knowledge and understanding that can, indeed, lead to new life."

— Jane S.,
wife of a sexual addict

"In this unflinchingly honest look at the complicated road to recovery from sexual addiction, Wheeler challenges the typical, unhealthy views of sexuality that our culture promotes and offers support for those who courageously choose hope in their struggle for freedom. At the heart of the story is a faithful God who is for us no matter how messy that struggle may be."

— **Steve Siler**, Director / Music for the Soul Producer / *Somebody's Daughter: A Journey to Freedom from Pornography*

"After working with many men stuck in sexual addiction it is great to have a book—*Now Choose Life!*—that not only deals with the topic head on, but offers tools that can be used to defeat the addiction, as well as help the family heal. *Now Choose Life!* is a must read for anyone dealing with sexual addiction or people that are helping others through it."

—**Rex Tignor**, Man Up Ministries

"Wendy and I are passionate about marriage and we have seen just about every area of dysfunction and stronghold that rips marriages and families apart. One of the biggest and most common issues we deal with is pornography addiction. It is not uncommon for a man to be trapped by porn before he gets married and believe that he is going to "just quit" after he gets married, only to learn that he is now, not only trapped by the addiction, but also being crushed by condemnation. The devil has spun a web that he begins to believe he can never get free from. I know all this all too well because the man I just described was me.

Wendy experienced this in her first marriage and, as she tells men today, it was the beginning of the end. She was deeply wounded and then was easily discarded, which led to her bringing baggage into our relationship. Thankfully, with God's help she nor I had to experience another failed marriage. *Now Choose Life!* graphically explains the damaging effects of the poison of pornography. It is a tremendous resource in the "Battle" to save God's men and to heal marriages. We look forward to adding *Now Choose Life!* to our list of recommended reading for couples in crises."

—**Michael and Wendy Behar**, Founders of Unlimited Discipleship Ministries

Now Choose Life!

*One Man's Journey
Out of the Grip of Pornography*

Janet K. Wheeler

*With Recollections and Epilogue
by Bruce Wheeler*

Bluewins
Publishing

All scripture quotations, unless otherwise indicated, are taken from the Holy Bible, New International Version®, NIV®. Copyright ©1973, 1978, 1984, 2011 by Biblica, Inc.™ Used by permission of Zondervan. All rights reserved worldwide. www.zondervan.com The "NIV" and "New International Version" are trademarks registered in the United States Patent and Trademark Office by Biblica, Inc.™

I See the Lord, Andy Park & Mark McCoy ©1995 Mercy/Vineyard Publishing (ASCAP) Admin. in North America by Music Services o/b/o Vineyard Music USA. All Rights Reserved. Used by Permission.

NOW CHOOSE LIFE!
Copyright © 2013 by Janet K. Wheeler
Published by Bluewins Publishing
Bellingham, Washington 98225

All rights reserved. No portion of this book may be reproduced in any form without the written permission of the author.
ISBN-13: 978-0615741314
ISBN-10: 0615741312

*Dedicated to my husband, Bruce, who had
the courage and perseverance to
face the greatest pain,
confusion and fear of his life twice—
the first time because he had no choice,
and the second because God showed him that
revisiting it was the only way to find true freedom.*

*I am so blessed to have you
as my partner in both life and ministry!
You are an inspiration to us all.*

Table of Contents

Acknowledgments 11

Forward 13

Introduction 15

Now Choose Life! *Deuteronomy 30:11-20* 19

Part One: *Sliding on a Slippery Slope*

   1. Something's Wrong—I Think It's Me. 23
       The Roots of Sexual Addiction

   2. I'm Going to Hell. I Know I Am. 31
       Discovering Masturbation and Shame

   3. Whoa . . . the Answer? 35
       Introducing a Visual Component

   4. Girls, Girls, Girls. 41
       What's Normal—is it Mom or the "Bad" Girls?

   5. What's Love Got to Do With It? 47
       The Same Problem on a Different Coast

   6. Uncle Sam Wants ME? 53
       A Victim's Beliefs Are Confirmed

   7. Is THAT All There Is? 61
       A Disappointing First Experience

   8. All I Need is a Good Woman! 67
       An Illness, a Marriage and Dashed Hopes

   9. No Room for Two 73
       Old Habits with a New Spin, but the Same Old Sin

  10. Too Much, but Never Enough 79
       New Highs Bring New Lows

  11. Truth Revealed in the Strangest Place 87
       The Problem Verified

  12. The Denial That Ended Denial. 97
       Denying Christ on the Way to Surrender

Part Two: *Grasping for a Lifeline*

13. OK God . . . but who?. 107
    Starting to Reveal Lifelong Secrets

14. New Hope; New Risks. 113
    God Brings Assurance and Helpers

15. Stopping the Engine.. 119
    Preparing to Look at Deeper Problems

16. War of the Minds... 127
    Learning to Feel Real Emotions and Recognize Truth

17. And Then There Were Three 139
    The Necessity of Letting Go to Move Forward

18. Finding Answers and Losing Everything........................ 147
    Saying Goodbye to a Marriage

19. Sex Talk at Church?.. 155
    More Healing Through God's People

20. Burned to Serve.. 163
    Losing the Shame that Paralyzes

Part Three: *Finally Discovering the Path to Life*

21. What God Promises, He Does 171
    God Restores What the Locusts Have Eaten

22. Turning to an Old Friend... 185
    A Little Lapse Creates a Big Obstacle

23. Death Revisited.. 191
    More Lessons to Learn—This Time Together

24. Preparing to Take Back Our Men 205
    God begins to reveal His plan

25. Rocky Roads and Thoroughfares 217
    Rough Times and New Revelations as a Couple

26. But Wait . . . There's More!... 233
    Pursuing Healthy Sexuality

27. As For Me . . . I Choose Life! 243
    Leaving the Addiction Behind and Finding Real Freedom

Epilogue: *A Message from Bruce*.. 251

Endnotes 253

Acknowledgments

This book would never have become a reality without the help and support of three groups of very special people God has brought into, and through, our lives:

Family and Friends—
I want to thank my friend, Leah Puhlman for initially encouraging me to share our story with the world; providing accountability and feedback throughout the lengthy writing process; and offering her mountain cabin to us for a weekend of uninterrupted writing when distractions threatened to derail the project.

I am also grateful to Kip McCormick and Dr. Chuck Stecker for their unfailing support, constructive ideas and encouraging words.

And, most importantly, I want to thank Kathy, Bruce's first wife, for trusting us to tell what has been her story as well. We pray that God will richly bless her for being willing to let us share some of her most private and painful moments so that others can find encouragement and help.

Counselors —
Without the assistance of a God-choreographed procession of skilled professionals, it is unlikely that Bruce would have ever found

the freedom he knows today. We'll forever be grateful for the part that three very special counselors played in his healing journey.

Each brought a unique component to the table—Gwen made it safe for him to disclose the true nature of his struggle for the very first time; Emily was integral in helping him slow the engine of addiction down so he could finally begin to look at the underlying issues, and Karolyn led him through the difficult task of surrendering his life, wounds, and false beliefs into God's capable hands.

Co-Ministers of Truth —

Of all the things we've heard or read, three ministries and their special ministers stand out as pivotal in our own life and ministry. We owe a debt of gratitude to each of them:

Michael Dye—whose ground-breaking Genesis Process program has become the foundation for our Life More Abundant groups and our own ongoing recovery.

David Olson – for teaching us how to experience two-way communication with God through Listening Prayer. His instruction has changed both our lives and our ministry.

Andy & Annette Comiskey and the others at Desert Stream Ministries — for showing us the wonderful things that God can accomplish through wounded healers.

And finally, we also want to thank every man that has had the courage to be honest about his sexual struggles and recovery challenges. They are ministers in their own right. Their words have taught us much and they have been a constant source of support for Bruce in his ongoing recovery journey.

Forward

America has become a "porn nation." By some accounts, over 90% of all pornographic materials are made in the United States and over 90% of the U.S. porn is made in the county of Los Angeles. The results of a nation-wide addiction to porn is more than devastating—it is catastrophic!

The destruction of the masculine soul of men is destroying not just the men—but marriages and families. In addition, addiction to porn has become a generational curse being passed from the fathers and older men in the family to the next generations of boys becoming men.

The fact that addiction to pornography is a national issue does not really address the fact that addiction to pornography is a very personal issue. It is not just destroying lives and families—it may very well be trying to destroy *your* life and *your* family.

Last year I was introduced to Janet and Bruce Wheeler who felt led to share the story of addiction, recovery and healing from the perspective of a couple—not just a man with a problem who needed to find a solution or lose his wife and family.

Rarely is the reader allowed both sides of the issue without being forced to read two or more books. *Now Choose Life!* is the rare exception.

NOW CHOOSE LIFE!

Now Choose Life! is not just Bruce or Janet's story; it is *their* story, bravely made public with the hope another family could find healing and restoration.

I had the privilege of walking with Janet and Bruce as this book was being developed and written. They are not celebrities or superstars by the world's standards but are two people who have been, and continue to be, on a journey. They could be your best friends or next door neighbors. You could easily say the Wheelers are a couple just like most of us.

For the record, I believe the Wheelers are Superstars in God's heart.

I not only pray that God will use *Now Choose Life!* to transform lives, marriages and families—I believe God wants to transform our nation from a "porn nation" to "His nation."

God tells us in His Word,
*"This day I call heaven and earth as witnesses against you that
I have set before you life and death, blessings and curses.
Now choose life, so that you and your children may live and that you
may love the Lord your God, listen to his voice, and hold fast to him."*
(Deuteronomy 30:19-20a)

The war against marriages and families is raging. Pornography is at the heart of this battle. You hold in your hands a manual for victory, healing and restoration. Your choice is as it was when God first spoke the words.

**Before you are life or death, blessings or curses—
Now Choose Life!**

Dr. Chuck Stecker
President/Founder
A Chosen Generation
The Center for InterGenerational Ministry

Introduction

It is estimated that a *minimum* of 25% of Christians struggle with some sort of compulsive sexual behavior that is negatively affecting their lives and relationships. Some researchers suggest that this number could even be as high as an unfathomable 70%. No one seems to be immune—not Sunday School teachers, deacons or even pastors.

Even though the shame and secrecy surrounding sexual struggles make it difficult to determine the exact number of people that are affected, there is no denying that a significant number of our close friends, family members, and fellow worshippers are trapped in a life of overwhelming hopelessness. They regularly risk their marriages, careers, personal reputations, and even their very lives to continue in pursuits that no longer satisfy them, but yet they seem powerless to quit.

Repeated failures have lead many to believe that there is something inherently wrong with them—that they are somehow uniquely sinful and have willfully ventured beyond the reach of God's grace and forgiveness. They have all but given up the hope of conquering this thing that controls them.

My husband was one of those people. When, at 10 years old, he found someone's pornographic magazines that had been carelessly discarded in the bushes, he had no idea that he was embarking on a 45-year journey that would take him to despair . . . and back. It was a journey that, over the years, would cost him thousands and thousands of dollars, ruin his first marriage, and lead him to believe that suicide might be the only way out of the double life he was living.

Thankfully that was not the end of the story for him . . . nor does it need to be for anyone else that is struggling with these same issues. There is hope. There is freedom. There is restoration. And God makes it available to EVERYONE . . . no matter how far the spiral of destruction has taken them.

The road to healing is not an easy one—not for the struggler and not for the spouse. Much of the "help" that is available isn't very helpful. Harmful myths and even more harmful attitudes continue to magnify the shame and perpetuate the hopelessness that keeps people stuck. It is because of these challenges that we feel compelled to share our story with painful honesty.

By inviting others to walk with us through the retelling of the victories *and* the valleys that we've experienced, we create an opportunity for God's truth to replace some of the common misconceptions relating to sexual struggles and strugglers. We trust that our journey will become an inspiration and an encouragement to those who have not yet found the freedom and life more abundant that God has promised to all of us.

I never dreamed when I reached out to shake a stranger's hand in the summer of 1999, that I was saying hello, not only to my future husband, but to a new purpose in life. After an immersive and painful personal introduction to the heartbreak and destruction sexual addiction brings to lives and marriages, God began to place a burden on our hearts to share the hope and understanding He had so graciously given to us with those He would bring across our path.

In April of 2003 we started our first spouse's support group. A month later we began seeing some of their husbands as individual clients. As we became increasingly aware of the importance of peer support and creating accountability, we quickly turned our focus toward developing a group recovery program. We've been facilitating

Introduction

men's groups ever since, and have seen God do amazing things in the lives of those who have attended. We rejoice with each one that finds hope and healing, but, all the while, we are keenly aware of the unending sea of strugglers and their families who still suffer in secret. It is for them that this book has been written.

Each chapter offers a unique balance of personal testimony, practical information, and spiritual truth. Many of you will relate to Bruce's experiences, told in his own voice. Others will resonate more deeply with the frustration and pain that I speak of, as a spouse. Either way, it is our hope that by the time you have finished the last page of this book you will have gained a deeper understanding of the roots and progression of addiction and the ups and downs that are so very normal in recovery.

Above all, we pray that our words will help bring you the hope and courage you need to move toward the blessed freedom and abundant life that we have found.

Now Choose Life!

*Now, what I am commanding you today
is not too difficult for you or beyond your reach.
It is not up in heaven, so that you have to ask, "Who will ascend into
heaven to get it and proclaim it to us so we may obey it?"
Nor is it beyond the sea, so that you have to ask, "Who will cross the sea
to get it and proclaim it to us so we may obey it?"
No, the word is very near you; it is in your mouth and in your heart
so you may obey it.*

*See, I set before you today life and prosperity, death and destruction.
For I command you today to love the LORD your God,
to walk in his ways, and to keep his commands, decrees and laws;
then you will live and increase,
and the LORD your God will bless you
in the land you are entering to possess.*

*But if your heart turns away and you are not obedient,
and if you are drawn away to bow down
to other gods and worship them,
I declare to you this day that you will certainly be destroyed.
You will not live long in the land you are crossing the Jordan
to enter and possess.*

*This day I call heaven and earth as witnesses against you
that I have set before you life and death, blessings and curses.
Now choose life, so that you and your children may live
and that you may love the LORD your God,
listen to his voice, and hold fast to him.
For the LORD is your life,
and he will give you many years in the land he swore to give to your
fathers, Abraham, Isaac and Jacob.*

Deuteronomy 30:11-20 NIV

Part One:
Sliding on a Slippery Slope

The thief comes only to steal, kill and destroy.
John 10:10

1

Something's Wrong— I Think It's Me

The Roots of Sexual Addiction

Bruce's memories . . .

My problems with sex began in the crib . . .

I was, by nature, a sensitive little kid—one that just wanted to feel safe and loved. Even though I was born in the middle of a hurricane that tore the roof off of the hospital, everyone said I was a quiet, even-tempered baby. The problem was that that hurricane was not the only storm I was born into. Right from the start, our home was an unpredictable, scary place—especially for someone like me.

My grandma often told a story about how, when I was very young, I stayed with them for a few months while my mother recovered from surgery. She said it was so cute that every time I got in trouble I would scurry behind the chair where no one could reach me.

I don't remember that visit—I was way too small— but it is interesting that one of my most vivid early memories was of me hunkering down behind the worn brown couch in our tiny basement apartment. I couldn't have been more than four at the time, and already I had learned to hide when I felt afraid or insecure. Although I can't remember what caused me to burrow in that particular day, I do remember feeling so protected back there. The thick over-stuffed cushions muffled the crazy world I lived in. It was an oasis for my wind-up musical teddy bear and I. We were practically inseparable—teddy and me—so it was no surprise that he was close by my side whenever I needed a friend.

"Bruce, where are you?" I heard my mother call. At first she seemed like any concerned mother, checking up on her child. I didn't answer— I'm not even sure why. I hadn't been running away from her or anything—I was just back there listening to my teddy's tunes, but when she yelled for me again, I could tell from her voice that she was getting mad. There was no way I was coming out now!

I clutched my teddy tighter with one hand and reached for my genitals with the other. Somehow it soothed me to hold myself. I guess I must have done it a lot, because I remember my mother telling my dad that there had to be something wrong with me, because I was always touching myself.

"Bruuuuce! Are you behind that couch again?" You better come out from there right now!" Every word was sharp and staccato. "You're really making me mad. If you know what's good for you, you better get out here right this minute!"

I remember being scared—so scared. I could tell she was really mad and you never knew what was going to happen when Mom got mad. I could hear her getting closer. She yanked the couch out from the wall and came running at me with bulging wild eyes. I will never forget that look. She grabbed me and just lost it. She started wailing on me in a blind rage. I was so scared I could hardly take in all the things she was yelling at me as she hit me. Always before when she spanked me and I started crying she would stop, but not today. She just kept yelling and hitting. At one point I remember her calling me a pervert. I didn't know what that meant . . . but I knew it wasn't good. The word stuck in my mind. Whatever it was, I knew I couldn't be that or Mom wouldn't love me any more.

I was sobbing by now—partly because of the beating, but partly because I was so very, very afraid. When the hitting stopped, I remember being surprised that Mom was crying too. Still sniffling, I stood looking up at her, trying to figure it all out. She said she was *sorry and she didn't know what made her do that, and she would never do it again. I was confused by the things she was saying, but I was totally convinced that everything that had happened was all my fault. There was obviously something really wrong with me to make her hit me that way. I had no clue what it was, but mentally I made a promise to try harder. Maybe if I was a better boy she would like me more.*

When my mother left the room, I quietly went back behind the couch and tore my teddy apart. I tore his guts out with my little hands and left him there in pieces. I never played with him again. He had been my friend, my security blanket, and he didn't save me. He wasn't a friend anymore. The couch had lost its safety as well. I gave up hiding there and started hiding in my head, instead.

Killing my beloved bear was somehow tied into my loss of security. I never felt out of harm's way after that. It didn't even feel safe to be me anymore. I had to find a way to be someone else—anybody but the little boy Mom seemed to hate so much.

Janet's observations . . .

Bruce's childhood stories break my heart. They reveal an environment that is in such contrast to the innocent, protective home that I grew up in. It grieves me to think of this sweet little boy—barely more than a toddler–living in a constant state of fear and confusion, in the one place that should have been safe and nurturing for him.

Both of Bruce's parents had passed away before I met him, so I never got a chance to meet them face-to-face. I only know them through the memories Bruce and his siblings have shared about their growing-up years.

I'm struck by the fact that, in spite of all the problems, it's obvious that Bruce's mother wasn't an ogre. Her children describe her as a good cook and homemaker. She loved to sing and give gifts, but, sadly, she also had a lot of unresolved anger (particularly toward men) that regularly spilled out on her family.

NOW CHOOSE LIFE!

Their father, on the other hand, was an easy-going man. He liked poetry and nature and taught his children that the really valuable things in life aren't things money can buy. Instead of being confrontational like his wife, he usually chose to avoid difficult situations and feelings, which caused him to be emotionally distant and often physically absent. Although he never seemed to be able to get ahead financially, he worked long hours and, when he wasn't at work, he was most often away from his family somewhere hunting or fishing.

Together they were like oil and water. They were the epitome of the "city girl" and the "country boy"—an unlikely pair that pushed each other's buttons on a pretty regular basis. She wanted a life of security and culture and he had a deep yearning for adventure. His inability to provide what she had hoped for seemed to further fuel her resentment of men.

Even though early family photographs show his parents as a loving young couple, Bruce recalls that his mother always seemed to be mad at their Dad about something. There were lots of fighting and harsh words in the Wheeler house. His mother would say awful things about men in general, and her husband in specific, with little thought that impressionable young children were listening.

People often think that the children are too young to comprehend what they are talking about, so it really doesn't matter what they say in front of them. Although it may be true that they are too young to fully understand, they are still taking it all in and trying to make some kind of sense of it, just like Bruce was. They can read the emotion and tone of a conversation, even when they don't fully grasp the meaning of the words that are being said.

I'm told that things weren't always bad growing up, though. Sometimes the family would sit and joke and laugh together. But it was impossible to ever fully relax, because there was no way of knowing what or when things would turn ugly. Often, late at night, Bruce remembers lying in his bed and hearing the whispers start. Panic would set in because he knew that the hushed words would intensify and soon his parents would be screaming and throwing things. Most of the time his dad would ultimately end up running out the door, jumping in the car and racing off down the street burning rubber and squealing tires, leaving his children behind with his raging wife. Bruce always feared that his dad might not come back alive or that his mother would kill them all while he was gone, as she'd once threatened.

The next morning, at the breakfast table, it was always business as usual. No one ever spoke of the arguments that had occurred just hours before. It was embarrassing to leave the house knowing that the neighbors around them had undoubtedly heard the whole thing. To this day, Bruce doesn't know if his siblings felt the same fears and shame as he did, or whether they were able to find ways to tune it out and not let it affect them as deeply as it did him. No one has been willing to be the first to break the unwritten family rule of silence.

Throughout his childhood, Bruce grappled to understand his mother's volatile temper and the steady stream of negative messages he received about his sexuality, gender and acceptability as a person. Sex seemed to be a horrible thing that brought about angry accusations and threats against his father and other men. Among other things, he was told that "men are bastards that will say anything to get sex" and "men hurt people with sex." He swung between being angry with his mom for saying such horrible things about his father and his own gender, and trying desperately to assure her that he would never be like those men she talked about. He was convinced that if he could just be different than other men, he would be able to earn her love.

Even before he understood what sex was, it had become something bad and hurtful. It wasn't the only thing he had difficulty understanding, however. Other puzzling encounters intensified the confusion he was already feeling about so many things in his young life. His innocent attempt to make friends with a neighborhood girl, when they were four or five, came to an abrupt end, when his mother discovered that he had ventured down the street to play at her house. He could never understand why she came and drug him home, forbidding him to ever play with her again. When he asked her why, she said "boys don't play with girls." It just didn't make sense to him. She was a nice girl that he enjoyed playing with, but he was being told she was "different" and being with her was bad.

Even though he was quieter, Bruce's dad was not without his own opinions about what was good and bad; acceptable and not, especially when it came to masculinity. The men he spent most of his time with were primarily World War II veterans and hunting buddies, and it is obvious that their views of manhood, defined by a tough, self-sufficient camaraderie, significantly affected the message he passed on to his sons.

Prevalent thinking like "Men don't show emotion"; "Always be ready to fight for 'the cause'"; "Sex is something to joke about"; and "There's something 'funny' about a man who seems too sensitive" wreaked havoc on a gentle young boy's feelings of acceptability as a male.

A loving little four-year old also had a hard time understanding why his father would shove him off his lap saying "men don't touch men" when he innocently tried to crawl up and give him a hug. It was equally confusing a few months later when he came home crying about a bully in the neighborhood that threatened to beat him up and his father responded by telling him "I don't care whether you win or lose, but if you don't fight back next time, I'll beat you up myself." Bruce didn't want to fight . . . but when, out of fear of failing his father, he did, it felt good to hear his Dad proudly relating the story of his son's altercation to his cronies. Unfortunately, these messages that were meant to make Bruce tough just magnified the feeling that there something inherently wrong with him.

Although coming to terms with what was expected of him as a male was a primary source of confusion, girls continued to be an enigma, as well. As he moved through grade school Bruce found he was drawn to them—infatuated with them—but every time he got near them he seemed to get in trouble. He didn't see it happening that way for any of his friends—only him—and he couldn't figure out why. He remembers asking his mother once if he could go bike riding with a neighbor boy. She agreed and they rode off. Their adventure lead them a few miles away to the neighborhood of some girls his friend knew. The boys ended up talking and showing off for the girls. It was pretty innocent, age appropriate stuff, but it wasn't long before Bruce caught sight of his Mom AND Dad pulling up beside them in the car. He could tell by the look on their faces that they were mad.

His dad got out, grabbed the bike and angrily threw it into the back of the car, while Bruce, feeling totally humiliated, climbed into the back seat. Once again he couldn't understand his parent's anger. He had asked to go. His mother said it was OK. He wasn't doing anything wrong. But, on the way home his parents called him horrible, and talked about what they should do about this boy who liked girls so much. He determined then and there that it was unsafe to let his parents see his interest in girls—it had to be a secret. It was just one of a lot of secrets over the years.

We've seen time and time again in the recovery groups that we facilitate that it only takes a handful of incidences in a person's life to change the way they think about how the world works . . . and how they fit in that world. Studies have repeatedly shown that a child's early childhood experiences set the stage for just about every belief and behavior they have in adulthood. Bruce's experiences told him that sex was bad, men were bastards, relationships caused pain and girls were taboo. Not exactly the stuff that creates a healthy sexuality.

2

I'm Going to Hell.
I Know I Am.

Discovering Masturbation and Shame

Bruce . . .

Everyone has someone in their life that comes alongside them and teaches them the "facts of life." My friend, John, was that person for me. In looking back I realize that not everything he said was all that factual, but at the time I was in awe of his wealth of "knowledge".

We met in grade school and were best friends until I moved across the country at age 16. He was a little crazy, but I liked him a lot. We hung out together. We hunted and fished together. We egged the Vice Principal's house together. We got drunk the first time together. . . but, it didn't seem to matter what else we were doing—his favorite pastime was talking about sex. He talked about sex and girls all the time.

When we went to the beach, he would point out what he was sure were butt prints in the sand and tell me that's where someone "did it" the night before. He told me about prostitutes. "Yea, really," he said, " You pay them $5 and they have sex with you." And . . . he told me about masturbation.

We were walking home from school one spring day. We were dawdling along, in no particular hurry, as eleven-year-olds have a way of doing, when out of the blue he turned to me and asked, "Have you ever gotten a hard-on?" I looked away. I was so embarrassed I didn't even answer, but John didn't seem to notice—he just kept on talking. "Ya know, if you touch it and play with it when it's hard it feels REALLY good. Ya just hold it and rub up and down."

Usually I would never dare do the things John talked about—like grabbing girls' butts and snapping the backs of their bras—but there was something about this new idea that was really intriguing. To tell the truth, I could think of little else all the rest of the way home. I felt really drawn to try it—but how could I get away with it when I shared a bedroom with my older brother? I certainly couldn't let him know about it. In fact, I remember somehow instinctively knowing that this had to be a secret. NO ONE could know about it.

A few nights later, when I was sure my brother was asleep, I found the opportunity I had been looking for. I felt shame before I even did anything, I remember thinking that it sounded really bad—definitely not something good boys would do—but my curiosity got the best of me.

Touching and rubbing felt good right from the start. It kept getting better and better. Oh my goodness . . . what's going on? My whole body was involved, like the reverberations of an explosion. I was scared. I didn't know anything about semen or orgasms—and I certainly didn't know what was happening to me. Whoa! Incredible! . . . but oh, so scary! Mom was right. I WAS bad. I WAS evil. I was going to hell and nobody could know about it.

Yes, I knew beyond a shadow of a doubt that I was going to hell, but, I also knew I wanted more. I was hooked already.

Janet . . .

Some men we have talked to are surprised when Bruce tells them that he knew he was addicted from the very first time he masturbated, but that was the truth for him. For others, sexual addiction is a more gradual process, but, given the right conditions, it will take hold of every life and it won't let go.

According to a number of scientific studies, some people seem to be pre-wired for particular addictions. They appear more vulnerable to a compulsive behavior or substance than other people. Brain scans actually show a different level of activity from the first introduction of that substance in those with this predisposition. This does not mean that the person is powerless to avoid addiction, but it may explain why some people become so easily and quickly addicted.

For Bruce, masturbation instantly became a daily ritual. Right from the start he would masturbate two or three or even four times a day. He said it felt like the perfect answer to the internal struggle between his awakening hormones and the early messages he had received about the evils of sex and women. He could take care of his growing sexual desires without having to worry about the dangers that he, after watching his parents interact, was convinced were a part of all real relationships.

It was easy at first—the underwear section of the Sears catalog; a thought about one of the girls at school; fantasies about the $5 prostitutes that John had told him about—it didn't take much "inspiration" to get him going. All he needed to do was think about something sexual to begin the process.

Masturbation became a way for Bruce to escape from reality. In a home where there were ample reasons to want to find an escape, he masturbated in bed almost every night—except for when his mom and dad were fighting. Even though his parent's fights were something he desperately longed to avoid, the overwhelming fear that an already explosive situation would get so out of control that he or other family members might be in danger of losing their lives left little room in his brain for fantasies.

During the day, when he wasn't at school, he started spending more and more time in the bathroom with his new diversion. His family, believing he was just dawdling and being selfish with their only bathroom, regularly pounded on the door and yelled that he needed to speed it up. Although their constant interruptions were sometimes a bit unsettling, he kept his wits and remained exceedingly careful to never let anyone actually catch him "in the act". He was completely convinced that if anyone knew what he was doing, they wouldn't love him anymore.

Bruce describes fighting a horrible inner battle right from the beginning. He was sure that what he was doing was wrong, and even evil, but yet he couldn't make himself stop going back for more. Masturbation elicited the worst feelings and the best feelings all at the same time. It intensified the disgust and self-hatred he felt toward himself, but yet, in some weird way, it made things more tolerable.

As a mom, I can't help but think back to when my own son was ten or eleven. My memories are of him playing with action figures and Transformers and having his first crushes on the girls in his class—appropriate pre-teen pursuits . . . and yet, this is the same age when Bruce and so many others start grappling with very adult issues and the very intense feelings of sinfulness and shame that often accompany them. Added to the initial fears and misinterpretations about life that Bruce had acquired growing up, they snuffed out any remnants of safety and innocence that should have been his at this point in his life.

In the frantic quest to make all of the bad feelings go away, Bruce would masturbate even more—sometimes to the point of causing blood. It scared him to death. He worried about infection or permanent damage, but there was no one he could talk to. It was such a young age to be so alone carrying such a heavy load of pain.

His shame increased even more when his favorite grandma died. He was sure that, now that she was in eternity, she would somehow know the truth about what a horrible person he was—there was no hiding it any longer. It felt like he had lost the respect of one of the few people in his life that had shown him unconditional love and he hated himself for it.

A vicious cycle had already begun. The growing shame and feelings of evilness were actually strengthening the addiction, but the pleasure and escape he found, at least for now, overshadowed the fear and isolation he experienced.

He didn't know then that he had only scratched the surface of the powerful shame that he would carry for much of his life.

3

Whoa... the Answer?

Introducing a Visual Component

Bruce...

I was born and raised in a quiet little town in New York State just a stone's throw from the Pennsylvania border. At one time it had been a bustling canal, railroad and industrial center, but by the time I was born, things had slowed down and the canal system near where we lived had long since been filled in. All that remained was a worn path that had been used by donkeys as they towed barges through the canals. That towpath made a perfect shortcut between John's house and mine and we used it often.

This particular day I was riding my bike. I was almost home—I probably didn't have a 100 yards to go—when I happened to notice some bags tossed carelessly in the bushes beside the path. I swung my leg over the bike and coasted to a stop. I could feel my heart thumping hard in my chest as I gingerly peeked at the contents of the first mangled brown sack. I couldn't believe my eyes. Women. Beautiful Women. NAKED Women. Page after page of the most exciting pictures I had ever seen. I could feel a warmth beginning to build deep within my groin. I had traveled on this well-worn path hundreds of times before, but I had never seen anything like this. My hands were shaking as my curiosity spurred me on.

Wow, I must be the luckiest 11-year-old on earth. Someone had left these magazines here and I was the one that found them. How cool! For a few fleeting moments I felt like I was on the top of the world . . . like I'd won the lottery or something . . . but then a wave of reality hit me with a force that nearly knocked me over. I looked around quickly to make sure no one was watching. "Nobody can know that I have these. Where will I hide them? I have to have them. How can I get them into the house? Oh, boy, I'm REALLY going to hell now . . . there's no escaping it."

I didn't know then that the exhilaration is ALWAYS followed by shame. Unfortunately, it was a cycle I came to know all too well over the next thirty years.

Janet . . .

Men's attention is instinctively attracted to what they see. Whether they are channel surfing, flipping through a magazine or "checking out" a woman, they, by God's design, are very visually motivated. Women, on the other hand, have traditionally been more enticed by what they hear and touch. They long to know that someone is connecting with them emotionally and/or physically.

A male's propensity toward fixating on visual images, starts at a young age, Think about the last time you tried to get the attention of a little boy that was mesmerized by a bug or something on TV. It usually takes several attempts to pop them out of the trance-like state they're in.

As a young boy of only four, Bruce remembers staring at women in their underwear in the Sears catalog. It certainly wasn't a sexual thing at that point . . . but he still found something about these women interesting and attractive. He got enjoyment . . . comfort . . . pleasure . . . out of what he saw.

Even at this very young age, he was becoming keenly aware that there were significant differences between men and women. Not physiological differences (although they were definitely there too), but something more mysterious . . . something that they "had" that was off-limits to him . . . something big and, at that time, indefinable.

Whoa... the Answer?

In his daily observations, he became more and more aware of little evidences that supported his theory that girls had something special that he could never have. Increasingly he was encountering "taboos" relating to girls and "girl's things."

When no one was around he would sometimes sneak into his parent's room, open his mother's drawers and touch her underclothes. They were so smooth and soft. He was sure it was evil and bad— his father had always told him boys don't "do" soft — but yet, as a preschooler, he liked the silky feeling of his mom's panties and slips and seeing women wearing them in the catalog. He made sure that no one ever caught him looking or touching, but it was yet another internal source of shame and self-concern. Many, many years later, he mentioned it in a men's therapy group, and was surprised how many other men confessed that they, too, were confused and had felt deep shame about their early enjoyment of soft and silky things.

And then, at age eleven, Bruce stumbled upon a new caliber of visual stimuli and this time it WAS sexually charged. He discovered those sacks of porn at the exact age that most men later admit was the age they viewed their first pornography. It is a time of natural curiosity and changing hormones, and the enemy of our souls takes advantage of every opportunity he is given to set his hook and begin to reel these young men toward a life of spiraling destruction.

Those first magazines were pretty tame. Nude ladies. Butts and boobs. Nothing else. But, definitely more exciting than underwear ads.

Even though his daily masturbation sessions always happened behind the closed doors of the bathroom or in his bedroom after everyone was asleep, Bruce was too scared to bring the magazines into the house.

Instead, his collection found a home in the basement. Unless there was a hurricane or severe lightening storm, the storm cellar was used for little more than storage so its dark corners provided the perfect hiding place for "the stash." From time to time, when the coast was clear, he could sneak down and replenish his fantasies. It held very little risk. It felt safer than real girls. And, at first, it seemed like the perfect system.

NOW CHOOSE LIFE!

The problem with behaviors that become compulsive is that they are governed by the law of diminishing returns. This means that, as time goes by, it takes more and more of the behavior, or escalated behaviors, to get the same effect.

For the first few years Bruce didn't need pictures when he masturbated. Just thinking about the girls at school or something he had seen or heard about, was enough to get him excited. Eventually, though, as he started augmenting his natural fantasies more and more often with ones drawn from pornography, those old ways became increasingly inadequate. The more time he spent with the pornography, the less his imagination seemed to work once he walked away from it. Over time he began to rely on this additional "help" and started sneaking the pornography in and out of the house so he could view the actual magazines as he masturbated.

Once this became a necessary component of his daily ritual, it didn't take long to discover that once he had "read" a particular magazine a few times, it became less able to turn him on. The element of unpredictability and surprise was essential for him. If he put a magazine away for a while and then came back to it much later it would usually work again to some extent, but if he tried to look at the same images every day they would quickly become useless. He needed new material on a regular basis to satisfy his needs.

While he was still in his early teens in New York, he discovered that the corner store would periodically throw their outdated magazines in the garbage behind the store. If he worked it right, he could pick up a few new magazines there from time to time.

And, if he couldn't get his hands on anything else, he could always resort to Detective and Science Fiction magazines. Not only were they available at almost every newsstand back then, but at one point, when his uncle had been cleaning out his house, he had given Bruce and his brother a huge pile of them, along with some model trains and other "treasures". The magazines were full of stories about women with very few clothes on. Many of them included detailed descriptions of rape or seduction. No nude pictures, but vivid enough words and drawings to get a fantasy going.

Once Bruce moved to Washington State in his sophomore year of high school and got an after school job, his scavenging days were over. Even though he only made 90¢ an hour cleaning up the meat department at a local grocery store, his income was enough to keep him in a steady enough supply of fresh material. Although not quite as accessible as the internet is today, it was pretty easy to buy soft porn back in the mid-'60s. Nearly every Mom and Pop corner store had a rack of nudie magazines and no one even blinked an eye if a fifteen or sixteen year old brought one up to the check stand. If you had the money you could buy anything you wanted.

Even though the stores looked the other way, he was constantly worried that someone from his family would catch him. He knew what he was doing wasn't right, but he just couldn't let go of his fascination with it. It had a grip on him. His growing habit brought with it intensely conflicting emotions. Intense pleasure. Intense shame. And the intense pain of believing that people would hate him if they knew what he was doing.

All through high school, he hid his magazines around the house. Under the bed. In the closet. Just about anywhere he thought would be "safe." Looking back it's difficult to believe that no one ever stumbled upon any of it, but if they did, they never said anything.

Periodically, when he felt he was getting too much to hide or got totally disgusted with his secret life, he would throw it all away, only to start re-buying it a short time later. This pattern of purging and buying continued for the next twenty-five years. Even his most conservative estimates put a price tag of between $15,000 - $20,000 worth of pornographic magazines that were bought and destroyed over the years—a number that, in retrospect, is staggering even to Bruce, himself.

As a woman raised in the 1960s, it is difficult for me to fully identify with the strong enticement pornography appears to have for most men. Of course, I have seen pictures and read stories that I found arousing, but they weren't something I naturally gravitated toward. Words and caresses were much more exciting for me than blatant sexual images.

Today, however, the ease and availability of Internet pornography and changing societal views about "normal" sexual behavior are not only accelerating the speed by which men become deeply addicted to porn, but are also drawing in many young women who are increasingly finding that they, themselves, are becoming addicted to pornography. Their struggles are not with the romance novels or promiscuous sexual relationships that might have traditionally been thought to be the manifestation of inappropriate sexual desires in women ... but sexually explicit visual images—just like their male counterparts.

4

Girls, Girls, Girls

What's Normal—is it Mom or the "Bad" Girls?

Bruce . . .
During the years that my pornography use was escalating, I was also experiencing my share of crushes, heartbreak and anxiety about the "real" girls that wandered through my life.

For the most part I maintained a stand-offish, almost voyeuristic approach to girls even as I moved toward adolescence. The verbal and visual messages I had heard for over a decade made me more than a bit wary about getting involved in any type of relationship, but yet there was still something intriguing about girls that kept beckoning to me.

When I was about 12, I defiantly challenged my mother's rules and made friends with two of the girls in my sixth grade class. At first the friendship was fun and non-threatening. We just chummed around and laughed a lot together.

The two were almost stereotypical "trailer trash" kind of girls—a bit flashy and seductive. Even though they were nice enough, they definitely had an "edge" that I wasn't used to. At times they seemed to get immense enjoyment out of watching me squirm and turn red when they "came on to me" or flashed a glimpse of the garters and stockings that all the girls wore in the early sixties. I particularly recall one time when I was heading home after school. One of them happened to be walking down the opposite side of the street. It was a breezy day, and at one point, the wind caught the hem of her dress and blew it up past her waist. She turned and winked at me and asked if I liked her panties. Her unexpected response both scared me and turned me on. Embarrassed, I got out of there as quickly as I could and ran for home. For years, I kicked myself for not taking advantage of the situation. I was sure every other guy in the world would have . . . but the nice guy in me wouldn't—couldn't— do it.

Something changed over the summer, however. Early in the fall I overheard one of them talking at the next table in the school lunchroom about having sex. Even though she was barely 13, according to her account she was dating a 21 year old. She bragged that she had told him that she'd only go out with him if he'd "do" her. The whole idea made me sick to my stomach and our friendship started to fall apart after that. With all her talk (and I'm sure some action as well), she quickly got the reputation of being "easy" and, sadly, was pregnant by eighth grade.

In retrospect, I realize that the attitudes and behaviors of these two friends were pretty indicative of girls that had been sexually abused, but at the time it just provided a strange mix of uncomfortable and titillating feelings. I masturbated more than once fantasizing about my imaginary responses to their sexual innuendos.

My first real crush was on a girl named Darlene. She was very pretty and had such a great personality. I was amazed that when my friend John, had grabbed her butt, as he often did with the girls he encountered, she hadn't gotten mad like most of them did . . . she just turned and smiled at him. That fascinated me.

Darlene was one of those girls that was just naturally sexy and always wore extremely short dresses. I never actually got up the nerve to tell her how I felt, but I used to follow her home from school and admire her from a distance. She seemed so perfect. It was devastating when one of my friends told me she had tried to get him to go to bed with her. I was so disappointed. As soon as I realized that she, too, was sleeping around, I lost my first love, but, of course, I had fantasies about it and masturbated to that too.

My mother had been very vocal about how men hurt women with sex, but now it seemed that all around me girls were not only interested, but bragging about their frequent sexual encounters. It was all very confusing to me. Everywhere I went I seemed to run into blatant sexuality.

Even John's own cousin was a sex maniac. Sex was all she talked about. Now, granted, it was John's favorite topic as well, but somehow it felt different coming from a girl. She was 17—just a couple of years older than we were and she had her own car. That alone made her pretty hot stuff, but I stopped going around her after we were visiting with her once and she proceeded to show off some new pants she had gotten. I'm not sure where she found them, but for some reason they had zippers where the pockets would normally be. With her fixation on sexuality, it should have been no surprise, that she had no qualms about unzipping those zippers and showing us her panties. After that, just being around her scared me. In fact, I was fast coming to the conclusion that real girls were ALL scary.

My only positive encounter with a girl came just a few months before we moved away from New York. For some time I had had a bit of a crush on one of the girls that attended the community teen club that I frequented. The club sponsored a full calendar of wholesome activities for the town's teenagers. Among those events was an annual Halloween party. Somehow, in spite of my general fears about girls, I decided to ask Eileen to dance. When she accepted, I lead her to the dance floor. As luck would have it, the next dance turned out to be a slow dance. The lights were lowered, the music was soft and it felt nice to have her so close. Part way through the song, she put her head on my shoulder. The closeness and gentle swaying to the music gave me an erection. I was a bit embarrassed, but for once it didn't feel *evil. It was different. It actually felt good. It was a normal, healthy experience—one of the few I ever had with a girl.*

Later I asked her if she'd like to date, but she said she wasn't ready. I took that as a rejection of me, personally, but then, a little over a month later, on my last day at school before we moved out west, she came up to me with tears in her eyes saying how much she'd miss me and wished I wasn't going. I always wondered if my life would have taken a different path if my family hadn't moved 3,000 miles away right at that point.

Janet . . .

It has been said that we attract people that are at a similar level of brokenness as we are ourselves. Although he wasn't aware of it at the time, Bruce's childhood experiences had created a very wounded young man.

Looking back over his teen years, it is astounding that such a high percentage of girls that Bruce encountered displayed sexual brokenness of their own. It is only as an adult that he realizes that this was not a normal cross-section of young women. Almost without exception, these girls were overtly seductive and very promiscuous. It's hard to know whether there is truth that he was actually attracting this type of girls, or whether he only had eyes to see the girls that he felt had the potential of hurting him or proving his theories.

Any sign of promiscuity was especially scary. Bruce had already come to the conclusion that women just wanted to trap you and if you had a relationship with one of them it would quickly turn to pain. He had seen, firsthand, the anger and sadness in his parent's relationship and his own experiences with girls continued to be confusing, at best.

Having sex seemed like a sure way to get trapped. If they got pregnant they "had" you. The whole idea felt like a direct route to a painful life. His mom was a constant reminder that it was better staying away from girls and observing them from a distance.

Girls, Girls, Girls

Instead of learning how to find and interact with girls that had a healthier, more normal view of sexuality, he avoided the issue entirely by turning his focus to traditional "guy stuff" like hunting and fishing. It became normal for him and a few of the other neighborhood guys to run home from school, grab their shotguns, and head into the woods to hunt squirrels and other small animals until dark. To Bruce, guns seemed safer and more predictable than girls any day.

As long as he was unwilling or unable to reach out and see that there were other types of girls that weren't angry like his mother or overtly sexual like his friends had been, his beliefs about women remained unchallenged. In his mind there were only two kinds of women—mothers and "bad girls." His experiences had shown him that both of them were dangerous and that he was much better off hanging out with the guys or masturbating to sexual fantasies or pictures without any personal contact that would put him at risk.

The problem was that even though these choices felt safer, they didn't fill the deep God-given longing of every soul, including his, for intimacy.

5

What's Love Got to Do With It?

The Same Problem on a Different Coast

Bruce . . .
Just a few days after Thanksgiving in 1966, my Dad, older brother and I loaded up our family's 1960 Ford and headed down Highway 6 toward a new life. Even though Port Jervis, New York was the only home I'd ever known, we were painfully aware that if we wanted "something better" we were going to have to leave our sleepy little town. I will forever be grateful that, in spite of all the other mistakes they made in raising us, my parents were willing to make such a personal sacrifice to give my brother and I so many opportunities and experiences that they, themselves, had never had. I remember turning and looking out the back window of the car as Port Jervis got smaller and smaller and eventually disappeared in the distance. I wondered whether I would ever see my hometown . . . or my friends . . .again.

I was excited about our new adventure, but yet a part of me was apprehensive, as well. For the entire 16 years of my life, we had rarely ventured more than a few miles from home, and now we were moving, lock, stock and barrel across the country to Seattle, Washington and dad's new job at The Boeing Company. I had always dreamed of living in the Pacific Northwest, but now that we were on our way, it was devastating to realize that, as we drove through state after state,

I had no place to call home. I had no address and nowhere that I belonged. For all intents and purposes, I was homeless. In those days before cell phones and e-mail, if someone wanted to get a hold of me, they wouldn't even be able to leave me a message. I felt like a nothing—a non-entity. It was a feeling that gnawed at me all the way across the country.

Each morning my dad, brother and I got up before dawn and drove eleven to twelve hours straight, stopping only to grab a couple of quick meals along the way. Just five days from when we first left New York . . . on December 2nd we pulled up in front of my uncle's house in the Rainier valley just south of downtown Seattle. The first thing I noticed when I got out of the car was the strong and unfamiliar smell of the salty sea air. It was a pungent reminder that we weren't in New York any more.

By Christmas, my Mom, 9-year-old sister and 3-month-old baby brother had arrived by plane to join us and we had found a house to move into. A few weeks later, when Christmas break was over, my brother and I began classes at Foster High School in Tukwila. It was weird being "the new kid." In my family I had learned to melt into the woodwork because calling attention to yourself usually brought you trouble . . . but, at this new school, everything from my red hair and freckles to my "funny" New York accent made me noticeably different than the other kids. The feeling of constantly needing to be "on guard" combined with intense loneliness and homesickness, made it a particularly difficult transition time for me. That first year in Washington greatly amplified my already dismal view of myself and my value as a person.

In time, though, it did begin to get easier. I started to actually enjoy the more relaxed atmosphere of the West coast schools, lost my telltale accent, got a part-time job at the neighborhood grocery store and met some great guys that became lasting friends.

Unfortunately, as much as things were so different, in many ways nothing had changed. I still found myself regularly bumping into the same kind of wild, flirty girls on this side of the United States, that

What's Love Got to Do With It?

I had encountered so often in New York. Girls I barely knew tried to talk me into coming over to their house to check out their new bikinis or drop by their party with my sleeping bag; older girls in tight jeans came on to me in the line at the grocery store; and married co-workers talked with a wink about how boring sex was with their husbands and how they'd really like to get some "variety."

Each new encounter was exciting and scary at the same time. It was so confusing. My mom had said sex was bad and hurtful, but all these girls were blatantly flaunting their sexuality. On one hand it was embarrassing, on the other enticing. I was continually kicking myself because I couldn't muster the guts to do anything but fantasize about the situations.

When I was 17 I was excited when I got a job at J.K. Gill, a stationery and gift store that would be opening soon in the new Southcenter Mall they were building just down the street from our house. Being part of setting up the store from the ground up, was probably one of the most enjoyable jobs I've ever had. After the store opened I worked there off and on for the better part of three years. The crew was almost like family and many of us socialized outside of work on a pretty regular basis.

Nino was one of my friends from work. He was a few years older than I was and had already done a tour of duty in Viet Nam. His "worldliness" intrigued me. He dated a lot and had no qualms about talking about his many "experiences" with women.

The one thing I had that Nino didn't have was a car, so when the company held their annual Christmas party at one of the manager's houses across town, I offered to pick him up at his apartment. I got there a bit early so he invited me in and introduced me to his roommate and a couple of other friends that were evidently hanging out waiting to go to another Christmas party that was being held in their building somewhere. The air was thick with the smell of burning incense

Shortly after I got there, another friend of Nino's showed up with two very pretty girls in tow. Before anyone could even introduce him, he emphatically announced "Nobody better touch the blonde. She's mine." The girls giggled at his pronouncement and excused themselves to the bathroom.

When they finally came back—wouldn't you know it— that blonde gravitated straight toward me and started asking me questions about the artwork in the apartment. It made me incredibly uneasy. I didn't know a darn thing about art and I sure didn't want to get caught talking to some other guy's blonde. I tried to ignore her, but she just kept trying to make conversation. By the time I managed to extract myself from her questions, and turned to find Nino, he was on the couch, totally engrossed in making out with the other girl. A few minutes later I saw him get up and take her into his bedroom.

Feelings of intense panic started to build up inside me. I didn't know any of these people and I certainly didn't want to be here. I also didn't want any of these guys to get a glimpse of how uncomfortable and scared I really was with the whole situation.

Thankfully, Nino wasn't gone long. He emerged from the bedroom, saying "hey, guys, she doesn't want me to leave, she's still hot … anybody else want a turn? Hey, Bruce, how about you? Wanna go next?"

"Naw, Nino, we better get going." I tried to act nonchalant, but all I could think about was getting out of there. I felt an unbelievable sense of relief when I heard Nino said, "Oh, yeah, Bruce, I guess you're right."

In the car Nino couldn't stop talking about how hot his partner had been. He said he loved it when they just couldn't wait. He proceeded to provide more details than I needed to know, but somehow I could tolerate that kind of talk from Nino—it was just how he was.

I think, on one level, I was a little jealous that I couldn't be that open. When I told the guys at school what had happened, the common response was "I can't believe you didn't take your turn, man." I had already decided that deep down I was a coward. Now I was becoming more convinced than ever that there was something desperately wrong with me.

Janet...

As human-beings, we have a tendency to look for any data that will support the things we have already come to suspect about ourselves and others. It's almost as if we develop a special radar that is calibrated to receive only corroborating evidence.

During Bruce's teen years he was so busy taking note of everything that he thought proved there was something wrong with him, that he was all but blinded to his many positive characteristics and beliefs. The seed idea that he was bad or uniquely damaged had been planted very early in his childhood. Years of subsequent observations and assumptions helped feed those seeds until the strong roots of that belief began to permeate his being and rule his thoughts and actions.

It never crossed Bruce's mind that maybe the guys and girls he was observing were the ones with the unhealthy attitudes about sex. He never gave any consideration to the idea that his conscience might actually be directing him toward truth when something inside him told him that the kind of casual sex he was seeing wasn't right and wouldn't be satisfying. He didn't realize that he was showing integrity when he cringed at the idea of telling a girl he loved them to get sex like a lot of the guys he knew did. He didn't understand that he wasn't just playing a nice guy to get people to like him, he really WAS a nice guy. He was only able to assimilate the information that supported his erroneous beliefs. Everything else, even if it was true, was discarded.

At a time when most teens are trying to "find themselves," Bruce continued on the path of losing his authentic self little by little. The feelings of not belonging, not fitting, not being "normal" drove him further and further into emotional isolation and the safety of pornography and fantasies. The more he believed that he was "different", the less he was willing to show his true feelings and fears to others, for fear that they would judge and shun him.

This period of Bruce's life was particularly weighed down by internal battles. As a very young boy watching his parent's struggles, he had vowed that he would never get married, and yet there was a part of the teenage Bruce that was lonely and wanted a girlfriend. He had seen a few people that seemed happy in their relationships, but a much larger percentage of the couples he observed were fighting, complaining or visibly unhappy. He struggled with not wanting to be alone, but yet, fearing that if he did date he might get into something painful like his mom and dad's marriage. The fact that he didn't have much money or time for high school dances, games and dates provided a handy excuse (even in his own mind) for avoiding the risk of close co-ed interactions.

He also still struggled to understand the truth about women and sexuality. Part of him was reluctant to let go of the idea that girls couldn't possibly like sex because of his mother's obvious disdain for it, and yet everywhere he looked girls were flaunting it, offering it, or asking for it. He couldn't make sense of why pretty girls like the ones at Nino's apartment would actually want to be used in the way they were. How could sex be something special when there were a bunch of guys—even strangers—participating? Unfortunately, there was nowhere that seemed safe to ask his questions or explore his confusion and fears, so there could be no resolution.

It was only when any possibility of a sexual component was removed from a relationship that Bruce could relax and enjoy spending time with a girl. He often spent time with a couple of his other co-workers, one of which was a girl whose boyfriend was in Viet Nam. As a threesome, they could go out and do things together knowing it wouldn't go anywhere. They had fun. They went to Seattle center. They went out to eat. They just sat and talked. He didn't realize at the time that it was a good model of what a healthy relationship should be.

6

Uncle Sam Wants ME?

A Victim's Beliefs Are Confirmed

Bruce . . .
I graduated from high school in the spring of 1969 and entered Highline Community College the following fall, just a few months before my 19th birthday. I was still living at home, but since I was going to school, continuing to work part time at J.K. Gill to pay for my car and school expenses, and spending time with some of "the guys" from high school, I was rarely there. Life finally seemed to be getting comfortable.

Unfortunately, it didn't last long. My life took another unexpected turn on December 1, 1969, as my dad and brother and I gathered around the TV. That night they were televising the first draft lottery since 1942. The drawing would determine the order of mandatory induction into the armed services for nearly 850,000 men born between January 1st, 1944 and December 31st, 1950. With a November 22, 1950 birthday, I was in that group, as was my older brother.

Every possible birth date (including leap day, February 29th) had been put in one of the 366 blue plastic capsules and placed in a large water-cooler sized glass container. We watched anxiously as New York Representative Alexander Pirnie from the House Armed

NOW CHOOSE LIFE!

Services Committee reached in and drew out the capsule containing September 14th, the birth date of the men that would be the very first to be drafted. After that ceremonious start, the remaining numbers were individually chosen and read by a stream of young men and women from the Selective Services Youth Advisory Committees of the various states.

"April 24th...December 30th... February 14th... October 18th... September 6th... October 26th...September 7th... November 22nd...no... not November 22nd. It couldn't be! I had never won anything in my life and now my birthday had been selected in the top ten in the draft lottery? How unlucky could a guy be? Our country was in the middle of the war in Viet Nam and now, in just the space of a few minutes, a future in the military, and most likely that war, had become my inescapable destiny.

Suddenly my life narrowed to only two options: wait for the draft letter to come telling me to report for a two year stint in the army and an all expense paid trip to Viet Nam, or enlist for six years in the reserve unit of some other branch of the military. I remember asking my Dad that night what he thought I should do. His reply was "You're old enough to make that decision by yourself." His curt answer made me feel so rejected and alone. Here I was, facing one of the most difficult decisions of my life, and my dad wasn't even willing to offer any advice or help me think it through. I guess it was one of those " rite-of-passage-growing-up-moments," but it sure did sting at the time.

The fact that I was going to college would give me a student deferment for now... but my low number meant that I now "owed" Uncle Sam some military time before I could get on with my life. The deferment only delayed the inevitable and left a cloud of unfinished business hanging over my head.

The release of photographs of the war's bloody My Lai Massacre in November and the reinstatement of the draft lottery in December had prompted widespread outrage and increased opposition to the war among Americans. Many young people were incensed at the idea of being forced to fight in a war that they didn't and couldn't support.

Uncle Sam Wants ME?

Any hopes that the country held out that Richard Nixon would be able to deliver the quick resolution of the war that he had promised when he was elected in 1968, were dashed when American soldiers were ordered to invade neighboring Cambodia in April of 1970.

Anti-war protests increased, especially among young people. One protest by students at Kent State University ended tragically when four students were killed and nine others were wounded by the Ohio National Guard that had been called in to control the already volatile situation. The shootings lead to a nationwide strike by over 4 million students across the country.

When my brother and I tried to attend our classes at Highline, we were harassed by picketers and turned away by teachers that opposed the war. Over 900 colleges and universities across the country ended up closing for the duration of the student strikes, and the anti-war sentiment and political agendas that were increasingly permeating the scholastic community began to wreak havoc with my ability to apply myself to my studies. By spring my grades had slipped to the point that my student deferment was in jeopardy. I was given until the end of fall quarter to get my grades up or be drafted. Instead I made the decision that I would quit school in the early fall, enlist in the National Guard and get my military obligation behind me.

In the 1970s the National Guard was not deployed into battle as they are today. Their job was to protect our home shores. I had a strong sense that if I went to Viet Nam I wouldn't come back alive. I don't know if it was a premonition or not, but by committing to six years of weekend drills with the Guards I knew I would never have to find out.

In the fall of 1970, while waiting for a spot to open up in Basic Training, I went to work for the Department of Natural Resources. I loved being outdoors—especially in the woods—so when Rick, one of my old high school friends who already had a job at the DNR, told me they were looking for someone to plant trees for a few months, it didn't take much prodding to get me to apply. I spent that fall living in a motel in Monroe, planting an average of 500 trees a day and, attending drills for the Guards one weekend a month. Even though

NOW CHOOSE LIFE!

I hadn't been to Basic yet, we had to attend special classes to learn marching and other military disciplines.

When the tree-planting work at the DNR was over for the year, I went back to J.K. Gill to help with the Christmas season and then went on unemployment until I reported for ten weeks of Basic Training on March 2, 1971. Immediately after finishing Basic I did another 10 weeks of Advanced Infantry Training (AIT) where we fired more weapons, learned battle tactics and participated in jungle warfare training alongside the guys in the regular army, that were on their way to Viet Nam. The evenings were ours, so we usually went to the base beer hall to drink and smoke cigars. It's unsettling to realize that some of those guys I trained and socialized with didn't live to even see their 21st birthday and the legal drinking age.

In June, while I was still at Fort Lewis, my parents and younger sister and brother unexpectedly showed up one day in a moving van. They told me that they had decided to move back to New York. Their announcement not only came as a total shock, but also brought back all those feelings of being homeless and worthless. In just a few weeks I would finish my 148 days of training with nowhere to go. I briefly wondered whether I should switch to the regular army—at least it would give me a place to belong— but I, thankfully, managed to talk myself out of that idea before it was too late to avoid Viet Nam.

Even though this period of my life was filled with intense feelings of helplessness and resignation, I didn't masturbate at all during the whole time I was in active duty. I totally stopped the behavior. I'm sure it helped a little that the drill sergeants wore us ragged every day, but I was also terrified of being branded as one of those "fruit cakes" that masturbated in their bunks. I vowed that there was no way I was doing that there and effectively shut off my sexuality for nearly five months.

The longevity of my abstinence made it easy to convince myself that I really didn't have a problem with pornography or masturbation after all. Obviously, I could stop whenever I wanted. Or could I?

Janet . . .

Patrick Carnes, a pioneer in the field of sexual addiction, isolated four core beliefs that are common to nearly all people that struggle with sexual compulsions:

1. "I am basically a bad, unworthy person."
2. "No one could love me as I am. "
3. "My needs are never going to met if I have to depend on others."
4. "Sex is my most important need."

Most people—even those without sexual issues—can relate, on some level, to the first three items on this list. For some, these judgments are passing thoughts that come only at the most difficult times of life. For others the beliefs that they are unworthy, unlovable and alone have become so ingrained that they seriously affect both their own self worth and their ability to relate to others. The part that varies for each individual is the thing that they have determined to be their most important need. That need is whatever they have discovered helps them escape the pain that their beliefs bring.

Bruce's early observations and determinations that :

a. there must be something wrong with him
b. he had to act or be a certain way to be loved
c. people were unpredictable, and therefore, couldn't be trusted, and
d. sexual fantasy and masturbation could temporarily relieve his emotional pain,

were all natural precursors to these same destructive core beliefs.

Any time a situation intensifies one of our core beliefs, we instinctively seek out the thing that we have learned will soothe the accompanying painful feelings.

When Bruce, who already believed that there was something wrong with him, was chosen 9th out of the 366 possibilities in the draft lottery it felt like proof that he was not worthy of receiving anything good; when his father refused to discuss an issue that was of dire importance to him it seemed to confirm his belief that he was unlovable and always in danger of rejection; and when his family decided to move back across the country without warning, it solidified the idea that Bruce was all alone in the world. Although none of these issues had anything to do with sex or lust, they all lead to compulsive sexual behaviors, because each incident stirred up unbearable and familiar feelings of inadequacy and rejection.

When a new belief or fear is introduced that has the potential of causing more pain than the original feelings that the compulsive behavior was soothing, the old patterns can often be shelved for a period of time. For Bruce, the fear of being labeled a pervert or a weirdo while he was in the barracks was much stronger than the negative feelings that were generated by his initial core beliefs. While in this environment, masturbation no longer felt like a viable solution, and ceased to be a struggle.

This is a situation where the absence of the unacceptable behavior does not equate to healthiness or healing. It is easy for people to convince themselves that they really don't have a problem when they aren't actively participating in the undesirable behavior but, unfortunately, unless that person's core beliefs have been rewritten through intentionally reaching out to God and other people for help, nothing has actually changed. The behavior modification is only temporary. The triggers are still the same and eventually, when the situation is right, the old activities, or other new substitute compulsions, will surface again.

Deep down most sex addicts believe that without sex they cannot be or even feel normal. Sex is the thing that helps them get through the difficult patches in their lives. If, like Bruce, their other beliefs and experiences have taught them that relationships are unpredictable and risky, the sexual activity must be of a non-intimate nature like fantasy, pornography, strip clubs, phone sex, or anonymous sex.

If a person's behaviors escalate to the point that they become completely disgusted with themselves, or a new predominant fear is introduced, they may try to distance themselves from their undesirable activities by completely shutting down their sexuality. In this sexually anorexic state they attempt (often quite successfully) to avoid all sexual thoughts and activities. Sex becomes their most terrifying need. Instead of seeing it as an answer, they now see it as something that will open the door to pain, emptiness and shame.

If their sudden lack of interest in sex begins to cause tension in their marriage, they might also temporarily assume the role of co-addict for fear of losing the love of their spouse. For co-addicts (a role more commonly held by the spouses of sex addicts) sex has become a sign of love. As long as someone wants them sexually they feel that they are acceptable and lovable.

Promiscuous sexual behavior is often fueled by co-addictive beliefs. In these cases, a person's feelings of self-worth have become desperately entangled with their sexuality. Even if their encounters are, in actuality, only recreational sex devoid of real caring and intimacy, the co-addict has been able to convince themselves that because someone wanted their body they still have value as a human being. Frequent sex becomes the price they must pay to maintain the feeling that they are loved.

As circumstances and internal motivations change, a person may fluctuate between addiction, anorexia and co-addiction. It just depends on which fear or belief has predominance at any given time. Each of these stances is equally harmful, however, and will ultimately leave the individual feeling powerless and depressed.

7

Is THAT All There Is?

A Dissapointing First Experience

Bruce . . .
What in the world was I thinking? Why did I ever agree to this silly blind date? Who in their right mind drives a hundred miles— right smack in the middle of the winter— to spend the evening with somebody they've never met? What an idiot!

The weather hadn't been so bad when I left Seattle—just cold and cloudy—but it was deteriorating fast. I wasn't even halfway to Bellingham when it started snowing. At first there were just a few fluffy flakes, but then it started coming down harder and harder. Each mile was worse than the one before. Thicker. Fiercer. Slipperier. It didn't take long for it to turn into a virtual white out. More than once I thought about giving up and finding a place to turn around. It just didn't make sense to be risking my life for someone I might not even like.

I was 22 years old and the only other date I'd ever had was when my sister-in-law set me up with a friend of hers the year before. What a disaster that was! I felt like a clumsy geek. The two of us didn't have a single thing in common. In fact, trying to have a conversation with her was next to impossible. Eventually I got tired of trying to fill the awkward silences and took her to a movie. At least we didn't have to talk there. But, wouldn't you know it—the stupid movie had a sex scene in it. Not one of those sweet scenes where the couple starts kissing and the camera pans away . . . no, not this one. They insisted on showing almost every darn detail. It was so embarrassing.

Here, I hardly knew this woman, and all evening she'd been acting like she was somehow better than I was, and then I had to go pick THAT movie. I couldn't wait to get her home, but yet I silently kicked myself all the way to her door for screwing up the date. I tried to call and ask her out again a few weeks later, but she said she had a cold and couldn't go. There was a part of me that was relieved. The other part felt like the biggest loser on the planet.

I guess I didn't learn my lesson though, because here I was plowing through the worst blizzard of the year toward yet another blind date. After Basic Training I had stayed with my brother and his wife for a week or two and then my friend, Rick had called to say that the Department of Natural Resources had an opening on a 20-man fire crew. I jumped at the chance and quickly moved into some barracks out in the middle of nowhere with the rest of the crew and fought forest fires for the rest of the summer. In September, after the fire season was over, I rented a room from Rick and continued on working with the DNR planting trees through November.

My parents were back in Seattle by then. I never heard the whole story, but I guess things didn't work out they way they had hoped in New York and they had found their way back to the West Coast yet again. I stayed with them through the winter months, working where I could, and when summer came I moved back in with Rick to do the whole DNR thing again. It was a guy's life. We spent our off hours hunting, fishing, drinking, building a dune buggy and doing a little pot. It wasn't bad, but it was a little lonely. Maybe that's why when one of the guys on the crew wanted to fix me up with his wife's girlfriend, I uncharacteristically agreed.

Our plan was for me to drive up and meet him and the girls in Bellingham for a double date, but I was having trouble even seeing the car right in front of me, by now. This was crazy! I started looking

Is THAT All There Is?

for an exit, but before I could spot one, the snowfall started to lessen and I decided I might as well keep going.

Boy, was I glad I did! This date was totally unlike my other experience. Kathy was warm and easy to talk to. Right from the start it felt like we'd been friends for years. The four of us went to a movie and then just hung out in the car for hours talking and laughing at Bunk's, an old-fashioned carhop-type drive-in restaurant. We had a great time. For once I felt like a "normal" guy. That date opened a whole new world to me. It gave me hope that maybe I wouldn't always be alone.

Almost immediately, Kathy and I started spending every weekend together. She was still living with her parents and I was, depending on the season, either living with my folks or some of the guys from the DNR. We worked it out so one weekend she'd come down to Seattle and stay with my parents, and then the next weekend I'd go up to Bellingham and stay at her grandmother's. Whichever town we were in, we spent all of our waking hours in each other's company.

After a few of our weekend visits, we started spending more and more time in the car kissing and making out. Once the initial awkwardness had passed, it felt good. I enjoyed snuggling and feeling our bodies respond to one another. I had never felt this close or safe with anyone before.

By late spring of 1973, we were getting pretty serious. Kathy and I had even started talking a little bit about the possibility of getting married some day. At the time, I was back living at home and attending college again for spring quarter while I waited for the DNR to start hiring for the summer season.

My parents and my six-year-old brother had moved again—this time into a small two-bedroom apartment—so space was a little tight, especially when Kathy was down. One particular evening, on one of our Seattle weekends, we were cuddled up on my roll-away bed in the living room watching Sci-Fi TV. My family had long since gone to bed, and the house was quiet, except for the drone of the television. We had been doing some serious kissing and things were getting pretty

NOW CHOOSE LIFE!

heavy sexually. Usually when things got a little out of hand Kathy would pull away and remind me that we had agreed that we wouldn't go all the way until we got married. I don't know why, but for some reason, she didn't stop me this time. Things just kept getting more and more intense and before I even thought twice about it, I was on top of her having intercourse.

The minute I orgasmed, everything instantly changed from exciting to yucky. A tidal wave of ugly emotions flooded over me. I felt shame because it had happened in my parent's apartment. I was terrified that they might have heard us. I felt guilty because we hadn't waited like we had planned. I couldn't quite figure out what had just gone wrong. I thought we had done the thing that would make you closer . . . and it just felt bad. I was so confused. I really loved Kathy, but I didn't like THAT at all. It reminded me of Peggy Lee's 1969 hit song, "Is That All There Is?"

Nino and the other guys were always talking about how great sex was, but my first experience with it was anything but great. Once again I had to come face to face with the conviction that there must be something inherently wrong with me. This was supposed to be cool and instead, it just felt incredibly yucky and disappointing.

Later, when we talked about it, Kathy admitted to some of the same feelings. She, too, felt guilt about not waiting; disappointment that it wasn't the big deal she had expected and sad that we hadn't made our first time special, we just let it sneak up on us. I guess I felt a little better knowing that I wasn't the only one struggling with it all, but deep down I still knew there was something more—the emotions that I had felt seemed much more ominous than simple first-time regrets.

Janet . . .

Considering all the fears and confusion about girls and sexuality that had accumulated during his growing up experiences, the fact that Bruce was willing to risk embarking on a love relationship is a testament to the depth of his desire to be connected.

Is THAT All There Is?

When, in the second chapter of the Bible[1], God determined, "It is not good for man to alone," he must have instilled a longing in his creation's heart to be in intimate relationship with another. Although modern society uses the word "intimacy" as a synonym for the sex act, its purer meaning is "to know and be known." In other words, to be truly intimate is to reveal yourself—imperfections and all—to another person and, in turn, to seek to know that person, inside and out, as well. The more we feel safe and able to be the person we really are (and vice versa), the more satisfied we will be with the relationship.

Kathy was able to demonstrate, more than anyone else in Bruce's life, a desire to know and accept him as he was. Although Bruce had a learned defensiveness that kept him from revealing many of his thoughts, fears and behaviors, he still could sense that this was a woman that could honestly embrace the parts he dared show her.

Unfortunately, that inherent desire to be intimately connected with someone did not magically erase all those years of being told sex was bad or the vow that Bruce had made that he would never be like the men his mother had talked about. Even though his family had not been particularly touchy-feely, his early negative programming had not extended to touching and kissing. Those activities still felt acceptable and even enjoyable. But, later, when his behaviors crossed the line into territory that his brain had defined as the forbidden world of "sex", his whole being—body, mind, and emotions responded with disgust.

Although the circumstances surrounding their first sexual encounter increased their shame and regret, even if Bruce and Kathy had waited until they were married, that line and those beliefs would still have been there and the outcome would have most likely been similar.

I can't count the number of people we've talked to over the years who have shared with us that their first sexual experience was a horrible disappointment. Even those who were successful in waiting until they were married often report struggling on their wedding night. Most people expect sex to be an exciting and wonderful event, like we see portrayed in the movies. Many of us, however, carry

NOW CHOOSE LIFE!

wounds and misinformation into our relationships that derail our chances of satisfying those expectations. Pornography, insecurities and childhood abuse can be especially damaging to our ability to experience healthy sexual expression.

Although everyone's experience may not be as profound as Bruce's, many people are confused by the fact that the sexual experimentation in their dating relationship is free and exciting, yet once they're married, it instantly changes in a negative way. This unwanted transformation often has its roots in the overheard opinions, societal views and negative sexual experiences that we have gathered early in our life.

Pride keeps most of us from talking about any initial disappointment or ongoing sexual concerns. Returning honeymooners that are greeted by friends and co-workers with "So did you have a good time? (wink, wink)" are certainly aware of what's being alluded to and would rather die inside than admit it didn't go well.

Even though as many as 2% of marriages are never consummated; an estimated 20% of couples have sex less than ten times a year[2]; and many others are silently suffering with a unsatisfying sexual relationship, we are terrified that we are the only ones that have somehow missed the boat to paradise. We are convinced that if we disclose any physical or emotional dysfunction we will be labeled as defective or weird. So, instead, we keep our fears and frustrations to ourselves and let our sexual secrets evolve into hopeless shame.

8

All I Need is a Good Woman!

An Illness, a Marriage and Dashed Hopes

Bruce . . .
March 23, 1974—my wedding day. Nearly 20 years ago I had vowed that this day would never happen . . . but here I was, waiting for the ceremony to start . . . and I was actually happy about it. Of course there were a few apprehensions flitting around in my head, but what groom doesn't have those at a time like this?

Sure, this was a serious step—a lifetime commitment—but Kathy was my friend, and that made all the difference. All the potential risks seemed worth it. She was soft-spoken and fun-loving—nothing like my mom. Even though it had been a long distance courtship, we had written a lot of letters and spent a lot of weekends together over the past year. We seldom even disagreed, let alone fought and screamed in the way I had seen my parents do.

I was more nervous about having to get up in front of everybody dressed like a goober in a suit and tie, than I was about our future together. Kathy and I had weathered a great many storms over the past six months. It had not been easy, but it gave me confidence in our relationship.

Our challenges had started late in the previous fall. One of my friends at the DNR was fired for taking the day off to help his mom move. I've never had much tolerance for injustice or inflexibility and, to me, this situation wreaked of both. There was no way I could just sit by quietly in the face of such unfairness. I needed to let my employer know how I felt.

Unfortunately, my little "talk" with the boss, didn't go so well. Things got a little heated and I'm embarrassed to admit that before the conversation was over I had called him a few choice names, thrown a radio at him and quit my job. That was the end of my career with the DNR.

With no job and only a hide-a-bed in my parent's living room to call "home," I figured there wasn't much reason to stay in Seattle any longer. Kathy and I talked it over and decided that I should relocate to Bellingham and move into the apartment she was now sharing with a girlfriend. It seemed like a great solution, so I packed up the few possessions I had, got a job at the Safeway and settled in with them. It was great . . . for a few months.

In early December my lower back started hurting. It kind of baffled me, because I couldn't remember doing anything to injure it, but the pain hung on for several weeks. Then, just a few days before Christmas, I came down with what I thought was a horrific case of the flu. I was sicker than I had ever been before—achy, nauseous, exhausted. I couldn't eat. I could barely even lift my head off the pillow. Even though I didn't know anything about the medical community in Bellingham, after a couple of days of feeling like I had been run over by the train, I picked a doctor at random out of the phone book and gave his office a call. I was relieved when they said they could see me later that same day.

Kathy was still at work, so I drove myself to the doctor's office. Even though I didn't have too far to go, it was a tough drive. I found it nearly impossible to concentrate on the road. The 103° temperature that the nurse noted on my chart a few minutes after I arrived, probably accounted for at least part of my inability to focus.

At first the doctor thought that I was probably right—that I had a bad case of the flu, but after examining me thoroughly and noticing *that the whites of my eyes were very yellow, he concluded that the pain I described having lately, had not been coming from my back, at all, but from my kidneys—a precursor to the full-blown hepatitis outbreak that I was now experiencing. I was in shock. It was several weeks before I discovered that some of the other guys in my National Guard platoon had also contracted hepatitis from tainted water in one of the drinking fountains at a weekend drill at Fort Lewis.*

There was nothing the doctor could give me for the hepatitis, so I was still so sick on Christmas Day that I couldn't even drag myself to Kathy's family's house to celebrate with them. Instead, I spent my holiday flat on my back, alone in my agony. A few days later my dad came up and took me home with him. Even though I was in and out of a feverish fog that first night in Seattle, I remember hearing Mom angrily insisting that she didn't want me in the house. My family had had preventative shots before dad came and got me, but even so, her fears got the best of her. It crushed me, that when I really needed someone, she wasn't willing to help me. Once again, I wasn't acceptable—even to my own mother. The next day, my dad obediently packed me up and took me to the hospital where I remained for nearly a week feeling sick and rejected.

Recovery was slow, but once I started feeling a bit better, another bombshell dropped into my life. Kathy's parents told her that they thought we were getting too serious and, almost simultaneously, my parents announced that Kathy was not welcome to come down and spend any more weekends with me. I'm almost positive that our folks never talked together about it, but all of a sudden, both sets of parents were insisting that we needed to break off our relationship. Of course, we did what any young couple in love would do— we started planning a wedding.

The fact that we were going to "make it legal" seemed to soothe both sides of the family a bit and they all, begrudgingly, supported us in our decision. Just six weeks later, here we were standing in front of 150 of our family and friends, pledging our eternal love to one another. The wedding went fine, other than the fact that I didn't even get to eat my own wedding cake. My battered system was still getting back to normal after being so ill and eating anything greasy, like frosting, would still give me bad pains, diarrhea, and burps that tasted like rotten eggs . . . not exactly the feelings I was looking for on my honeymoon.

We went just across the border to Vancouver, Canada and stayed in an elegant hotel down by the water the first night of our marriage. We were definitely out of our element amid the mink coats and tuxes. It was amazing to think that some of these rooms (not ours) went for as high as $900 at a time when the normal Motel 6 rate was, as its name implied, just $6 a night. Our extravagant expenditure was even crazier when you considered that the grocery store hadn't wanted me back after I got hepatitis and I'd been out of work until I found another job just two weeks before our wedding. We moved to a cheaper place the very next day, but we wanted our wedding night to be something special.

Unfortunately, the romantic part didn't go too well. Somehow I had hoped that it would be different now that we were married, but it still felt pretty yucky and disappointing. I quickly learned to disassociate when we had sex. I don't think I was every really present and fully engaged when we were being physical. No matter how hard I tried I just couldn't bring the feelings of love I had for Kathy into the bedroom. I was deathly afraid that if I didn't "perform", my new wife would reject me, so I learned to rely on old fantasies and mechanical responses to "do the deed."

Pornography hadn't really been much of an issue in my life for the past couple years. Ever since my stint in Basic Training, I hadn't had too many opportunities to engage in my old behaviors. It seemed like I was always living with a bunch of other guys or crashing on the hide-a-bed in my parents living room—neither of which were conducive to using pornography. My fear about getting caught continued to exceed my need to act out. Now, with nearly two years of "almost abstinence" under my belt, I was pretty convinced that I had simply outgrown that habit.

The feelings of belonging that I had been enjoying with Kathy also helped reduce some of the fears that I had tried to still with pornography and masturbation. Even though marriage made our relationship feel more secure in many ways, the fear of being sexually inadequate began to stir the glowing embers of old desires, once again.

Janet . . .

Most men believe that getting married will completely alleviate their need for pornography. They think that they only masturbate to "relieve their sexual tension" and once they are in a long-term relationship that provides the opportunity for sex whenever they want it, they will no longer have this requirement.

This may be true for a very small segment of the population, but it is wishful thinking for anyone who struggles with sexual behaviors that have become compulsive. Sexual compulsions are not about sex. At whatever point someone realizes (consciously or unconsciously) that sexual activity can make their internal pain go away, it ceases to be about sexual release and becomes a tool of survival.

In truth, most sexual activity is not about the sex act at all. In a healthy relationship, sex is about vulnerably sharing our innermost selves and feeling oneness with our partner. On the other hand, when it is used inappropriately, sexual arousal and release becomes a way to fill our needy places and anesthetize the pain in our lives.

Our brains are interesting. They have, built into them, a survival instinct. When something happens to make us feel afraid or uncomfortable it immediately seeks out anything that will take those feelings away and make us feel right again. When our brain begins to associate a certain activity or chemical with helping us regain normalcy, the seeds of addiction are sown. For many people, pornography, masturbation, or other sexual activity becomes that normalizer.

Even though Bruce loved his wife deeply, the feeling that he wasn't acceptable in the sexual arena re-engaged his old fears of being rejected by someone that was extremely important to him. Even though his young wife was willing and eager to enter into sexual relations with her new husband, he still began to crave the old comfort of pornography and masturbation, not because of the sexual release, but because, at least for a few minutes, it made his internal pain go away.

People—even pastors and other professionals— have been slow to grasp the difference between sex as an act of intimate love and sexual activity as a means of "zoning out", feeling adequate, or decreasing internal agitation and fear. It is unfortunate that both of these activities have been labeled "sex" because they are very different pursuits stemming from very different motivations.

9

No Room for Two

Old Habits with a New Spin, but the Same Old Sin

Bruce . . .
Back in the early months of my marriage I wasn't in touch with my feelings enough to know why I was being drawn back to my old habits. I didn't associate the familiar fear of impending rejection with my desire to lose myself in the pages of a pornographic magazine. I just knew that, after several years of near "abstinence", I had returned to thinking—a lot—about magazines, and naked women, and old fantasies.

At first it was just a few Playboys snuck into the house. Even though Kathy quickly became aware that I had them, I still hid the magazines, just like I did when I was a kid. I guess it might not make a whole lot of sense if you haven't lived it, but buying the magazines and getting them into the house without anyone knowing had always been an important part of the ritual. It added to the excitement and the sexual tension.

I'm not sure whether Kathy was just trying to be open-minded and supportive, or whether she hoped that it would kick-start our flagging sex life, but whatever the reason, she bought me a subscription to Penthouse for my birthday the first year we were married. Having magazines regularly showing up in the mailbox took away part of the delicious secrecy, but it did bring me a steady supply of new material and catapulted me into a whole new level. At first I would only pull out my growing stash and masturbate when my wife wasn't around. The opportunities were few and far between, but scheming how and when I was going to do it helped keep the excitement level high.

When that became too easy and too predictable, I started searching for something new to build the anticipation. I found it at the adult bookstore. I had always shied away from going into places like that. It just seemed too risky. But, when I finally mustered the courage to go, I found it to be both scary and exciting. Just walking into the store gave me a hit of adrenaline. My heart started pounding and my mouth got dry. I was like a kid in a candy store. Magazines, videos, sex toys—this was a whole new world. I quickly became so enraptured by what I was seeing that the fears took a backseat to the other feelings that were emerging.

The introduction of videos added a whole new facet to my growing dependency on pornography. It brought the women off the page and provided a new walking, talking, moving element to my fantasies. When Kathy discovered the videos, she suggested that it might be fun to watch them together. Our sex life was dying a slow death and I'm sure she hoped that it might help to rekindle the flames.

At first it did have that effect. We would watch the movies, get all excited and then have sex, but we never really talked about what we had seen or connected on an emotional level. It was just a physical response to what we had been viewing. We were having sex more—but I don't think it was satisfying the deep desire for love and connection in either one of us.

To make things even worse, I was becoming increasingly resentful that Kathy was "butting in." This was MY sanctuary. Her participation took away my control of the situation and diminished my ability to use it to hide from my pain and fears. It made me mad and began to drive a wedge between us.

Everything changed that spring, however. On Easter Day, 1975, I gave my heart and life over to Jesus Christ. Even though my parents had sent me to Sunday School as a child, I had never been told you could have a personal relationship with Jesus. Becoming a Christian gave me a sense of belonging that I had never experienced before. I was a "new creature" like everybody said I would be. I threw away all the pornography and thought my struggles with it were all done and over. I lived in a glorious pink cloud, basking in God's love for six months. I felt new and clean and free. Then I hit the wall. Almost overnight the pink cloud lifted and I realized that my sin was still there. I was devastated. I was sure that someone had lied to me. As I slipped back into my old behaviors, once again, I began feeling guilty and scared all the time.

What was the matter with me? Why was this awful sin still in me? I was convinced it was only a matter of time before God got tired of my constant failures and rejected me as well. I felt like I was living a detestable double life. I would go to church and truly worship the God I loved and then come home and watch dirty movies. I hated myself for it. I was ashamed and disgusted by my cravings and behaviors. I was terrified that someone would find out. But, no matter how hard I tried. I couldn't stop going back to those old behaviors time after time after time.

Janet . . .

Even though Bruce can't recall Kathy actually ever saying anything that would have indicated that she wasn't happy with him or his "performance", his struggle with the sexual aspects of their marriage had reawakened his old beliefs that he was somehow different, inadequate, and unacceptable, In the past he had always quieted the pain of those feelings with fantasy and masturbation. He, like anyone struggling with compulsive behaviors, was destined to repeat the same patterns as long as his original wounds remained unhealed and he had been unable to develop new ways to deal with those types of pain.

Unfortunately, each time he advanced to a new level of behavior, he was unable to find satisfaction in any of his previous activities. Even if he was able to abstain for a period of time, new cravings would be for the most extreme activity he had previously participated in. No matter how long that period was, he could never go back to the Sears catalog and begin the progression of activities all over again.

The deeper a person gets into pornography or fantasy, the less they will be able to be there for their spouse. If someone is masturbating multiple times a day or thinking continually about their fantasies or how to get their next "fix" they usually have little of themselves left physically or emotionally for their spouse.

When a woman begins to sense this distancing from her husband she often begins to question her own attractiveness and acceptability. She may have a desperate willingness to do whatever it takes to regain her husband's interest. If she has discovered that her "competition" is none other than pornography, she will most often respond in one of two ways. Either she will react with a violent disgust that multiplies her husband's shame and sends him deeper into secrecy, or she will attempt to join him in his "interests" in the hope that it will restore or enhance their relationship, as Kathy did.

Contrary to this hope, it is their spouse's made-up world of sexual images and fantasy, that helps them stay "stuck" and hide from the risk of true intimacy. As long as they are encouraged to settle for the counterfeit, they will never have reason to explore the healing process and the possibility of a healthy sexual relationship.

If you, as a couple are playing out fantasies, neither of you are being your true selves. The definition of intimacy is to know and be known. If a woman is recreating the images in her husband's mind (or vice versa), how can he ever get to know her true self, or her, his? To find healing, the person struggling with compulsive sexual behaviors needs to become comfortable with their God-given sexuality. Most fantasy will derail any efforts in that direction.

Compulsive sex without deep emotional connection ALWAYS leaves people feeling empty. Physical response is not the same as intimacy. It can never fill a woman's need to be seen and cherished or a man's need to feel normal and accepted and it will, instead, start to kill a part of their authentic self and lead to a life of fear and self-hatred. This is far from the plan God intended for their lives or their marriage.

10

Too Much, but Never Enough

New Highs Bring New Lows

Bruce . . .
If my life were to be compared to a roller coaster, my thirties would have to be the final "suicide" drop. Undeniably, there had been a slow escalation in the type and frequency of my pornography use through my teens and twenties, but it was in the thirties that my compulsive behaviors really got out of control.

Looking back, I can point to the very day that my thinking started to take a destructive turn. It was when Kathy told me, "I'll understand if you want to have an affair once in awhile. I know guys need that kind of thing. I just want you to know it's OK as long as it's just a physical thing. I don't think I could handle it if you were emotionally attached to another woman." There was a kind of sad resignation in her voice, as if she was acknowledging an inevitable pain that women were required to bear. Without even knowing it, my young wife, had just given me "permission" to take the restraints off my behavior. Something clicked in my brain and launched an intense internal battle that haunted me for years.

Even as I heard those words come out of her mouth, the moral part of me screamed inside my head" No, I can't do that. I would NEVER do that. I promised that I would never be one of THOSE men", but the addictive part of me seemed to be gaining a new and stronger voice that taunted me. "Oh come on you chicken shit . . . all you do is think and read about all this sexual stuff. You've never had the guts to go do it for real. You've had so many chances over the years and you've been too gutless to act on any of them. The videos and magazines are getting old. Kathy said it was OK. Go for it, man!"

I was confused and scared. I felt like I had been a kid happily playing within the playground fence. I had known where the boundaries were and in some ways there was safety in that. Now, in just a few seconds, the fences had all been bulldozed. I could go wherever I wanted. It was exciting. I had just been given the opportunity to explore the rest of the world, but it also made me feel unsafe and unsure. I didn't know where the line was anymore.

It wasn't something I thought about all the time. But it was a reoccurring mental struggle that became increasingly constant the more unsettled I felt. Pornography really wasn't doing it for me anymore. I was working swing shift by now; Kathy was working days and I had lots of time to myself—which I hated. Nobody bothered me since everybody thought I was sleeping. But more and more my "sleeping time", was being spent looking at magazines and videos and masturbating. I rarely got more than a three or four hour nap each day. The rest of the time was spent acting out in an almost trance-like state where hours would seem like mere minutes.

The more time I spent acting out, the more difficult it became to get a hard-on and a satisfying climax. The thing that had provided an escape for me for over twenty years had all but stopped working and I didn't know how to survive without it. I was starting to feel panicky.

Back when I began using porn so many years before, it had provided protection from the unpredictability of women. I could lose myself in sexual behaviors without any risk of rejection or entrapment. It felt safe. Now, ironically, I was terrified that these same behaviors would be the cause of my rejection. The trouble I was having responding to pornography was leading to trouble responding to my wife. I was petrified that Kathy would tire of our non-existent sex life and divorce me So, without ever resolving anything in my mind, I found myself desperately running toward anything that would help me function again.

My favorite part of the magazines became the letters that people supposedly sent in about their sexual exploits. Pornographic pictures started to take a back-seat to the tawdry tales about wild college co-eds, multiple partners, being seduced by a friend's mother and other forbidden sexual behavior My fantasies began to revolve around the narratives of these "real people." I started reading swinger magazines where people "advertised" for someone to fulfill their specific sexual fantasies. At first just reading and thinking about these people seemed to suffice, but over time, I increasingly toyed with the idea of acting out some of the things I had read about.

Little by little I began to cross the line my morals had once defined . . . kissing someone else's girlfriend at a party where I'd had a bit too much drink, spending time in strip clubs and x-rated movies, and wracking up hundreds and hundreds of dollars in credit card bills calling phone sex lines. Each new venture brought a higher level of excitement and increased arousal when it was new, but the effects always faded as it became more familiar. As I got involved in more risky activities, I increasingly felt like Dr. Jekyll and Mr. Hyde. I often had the sensation that I was on the outside watching myself do things that, at one point in my life, I would never have dreamed that I could do.

Eventually, the voice in my head started telling me that I was spending so much on phone sex that I might as well just go pay for the real thing. This was about the same time that several massage parlors opened in town that were rumored to offer a bit more than a therapeutic massage. It seemed like the perfect opportunity.

I thought about it a long time before I actually called and talked to them. My hand was shaking as I clutched the phone At first I just asked how much it would cost for a massage. The inflated prices they quoted me verified that they were not offering the normal muscle manipulation." Were there any 'extras' available?" I questioned. The *lady on the other end of the line assured me that they would provide additional services for tips. I was so nervous and scared that my mouth was bone dry and my stomach was tied in knots.*

I called dozens of times over the next year just to hear their voices, but always chickened out when they asked if I wanted to make an appointment. I told them I'd have to call them back later. At first just the idea that I might be talking to someone who "did other stuff" was enough to buoy my flagging fantasy life. It all felt so dangerous and taboo. Sometimes I would drive by the places. Getting a closer look and thinking about what went on in there was exciting. Sometimes I'd park down the street just before it opened and watch the women walk in to work. Seeing them increased the excitement even more. As I kept calling and driving by it eventually started feeling more normal to me—not quite the forbidden thing it started out to be. One day I finally got up the nerve to actually make an appointment.

The first time I went I only got a regular massage—I was too afraid to ask for anything more. None of the women ever came right out and said sex was available. Each session always started out as a typical massage. Eventually they would move down around your lower back, suggestively stroke your butt and legs a bit, and work slowly back up toward your crotch. They would get close—oh so close—to touching the parts that would turn you on, but never quite did. It drove you crazy. If you said anything about it they would indicate that there could be more to the service if there was more money.

Even when nothing illegal happened, the idea that I was in this place with someone who was willing to do more gave me a huge adrenaline rush. I couldn't believe I was actually here even thinking about this. On the next visit I couldn't resist their teasing and let them give me a hand job. Once it was over I felt so guilty that I vowed I'd never go back again.

In time, though, I forgot how ugly it had felt. The pornography still wasn't working and I had started feeling emotionally numb most of the time. I just wanted to feel SOMETHING. I made another appointment and this time I went all the way through with intercourse. It was very much "just business." We didn't talk or caress. She just got undressed and we did it right there on the massage table. The potential danger of the whole situation made the rush even greater. As disgusting as it was, I actually felt something for the first time in a long time. I was elated and relieved—and then the guilt crushed down on me. I felt such remorse about what I had just done.

Each new behavior left me feeling more guilty than the one before. I knew these things were wrong. They went against my Christian beliefs and my own moral code, but yet I couldn't seem to stop myself. I worried constantly that the phone sex companies would compromise my credit card information, or that someone would see me going in to a massage parlor, or that Kathy would find out about the money I was spending or the things I was doing. Going to church became increasingly uncomfortable as my "other life" became more and more difficult to conceal. I felt like I no longer had control. Even when the activities were no longer working for me I couldn't seem to stop.

In spite of the awful guilt, I went back to the massage parlor three or four more times over the next few months. Finally I couldn't live with what I was doing any more and confessed to Kathy that I had paid to have sex. I didn't know if she'd leave me or what, but I couldn't live with holding all that inside me any more. In spite of what she had said years before, she was devastated. I didn't think she'd ever stop crying. I never meant to hurt her. I felt such an incredible weight of guilt. I had a new understanding of the scripture in Matthew 5 about gouging out your eye if it causes you to sin . . .that it is better for you to lose one part of your body than for your whole body to be thrown into hell. Physical pain seemed like nothing compared to the intensity of the grief I was feeling. Something had died inside of me. I never believed that I could become this kind of guy. I couldn't believe what a sinner I was. I would even pay for sex. I was doing the kind of things that men do that are really perverted. I had broken all the promises that I had made to myself and my mother and turned into a man I barely knew and hardly liked.

Janet . . .

No matter what your compulsion, if you pursue it long enough you will ALWAYS end up in the same place: alone, scared, out of control, powerless, and hating yourself. You may be able to stop, slow down, or even just maintain the same level of acting out for a period of time, but eventually, both your need and your behavior will escalate. Without even realizing that it is happening, the thing that you once thought of as your savior and friend, becomes a controlling master that robs you of your power to choose.

Familiarity causes escalation. As we mentioned in an earlier chapter, when the brain gets used to a certain level of stimuli or behavior, that becomes the new normal. It then takes more or escalated behavior to give the same calming or numbing effect that the old behavior initially gave. Familiarity also causes a desensitization which can also lead to escalation. Things that were shocking or even repulsive at first become quickly normalized with repetitive exposure. The massage parlors, that Bruce initially found too scary to pursue, became less intimidating and more intriguing as he became more familiar with the people, the surroundings and the concept. We feel comfortable with things and places we have grown familiar with. We see this all around us—the mediocre politician that keeps getting re-elected because people know his name; the people who sit in the same pew every Sunday at church, the brands we consistently select at the grocery store—we are drawn to things we know.

We are also governed by things that are already familiar to us. When Kathy told Bruce she would understand if he wanted to have an affair, she wasn't saying she didn't care about him or that she didn't honor their marital commitment. The heartbreak she experienced later when Bruce admitted to his infidelity showed her true heart. Earlier in her life, however, she had observed women she admired standing by their philandering husbands. The idea that men "wander" and that it's just something women have to put up with had been planted in her mind. It was a familiar dynamic and therefore it seemed like a normal expectation to her. She didn't anticipate that when she was faced with the actual scenario she had talked about, her core emotional need to feel special and chosen by her husband would be stronger than her desire to "understand" what she had been taught were a male's sexual propensities and the price she had to pay to ensure that her marriage lasted for the long haul.

Many women have been given the mistaken idea that men must have variety in their sexual experiences. There is popular teaching that men have two different appetites—one for tender loving encounters with their wives and the other for raw sexual experiences. It purports that man's biggest struggle is with their lustful nature. This couldn't be further from the truth. It is this type of teaching that helps keep men trapped. After all, if lust is sin and lust is an innate part of a man, there is no hope.

In actuality, lust is nothing more than "sexual desire." It, in itself is not right or wrong. It is how we use it and who we allow to be the object of that lust that determines its sinfulness.

Contrary to much teaching on the subject, sexual compulsions are not an issue of sex or lust or bad choices, or even external behavior. It is about pain and loneliness and fear. It is only when a man begins to receive healing for the root causes of his behavior that he will be free to see and understand the healthy ways that God intended lust and sexuality to be used.

11

Truth Revealed in the Strangest Place

The Problem Verified

Bruce . . .

I stopped acting out after my confession to Kathy. No more massage parlors, no more magazines—no inappropriate sex at all. I went cold turkey. I was so incredibly fed up with myself, I could hardly stand to be in my own skin and I hated how much I had hurt my wife. I didn't ever want to see her in such intense pain again— especially if it was due to something I had done. I was optimistic that the memories of how painful it had been to confess would keep me from ever stumbling again. Kathy had graciously decided to give me another chance and I didn't want to risk screwing it up this time. I truly wanted to be the husband she needed me to be.

Although my behaviors had caused immeasurable pain for both of us, we'd also been experiencing another deep heartbreak throughout the seven years of our marriage. As much as we wanted them, we had been unable to have children. We sometimes wondered why we were being punished. It seemed like the couples all around us were having babies—but our turn never came. The unending frustration of the situation added to my feelings of being a victim and became yet another source of the misery that I tried to alleviate by acting out.

Fairly early in our marriage, medical tests had shown that both of us had issues that, together, would make conceiving very difficult. We tried a variety of methods to improve our chances, but ultimately they only added to our stress and made our sex life forced and mechanical. We were overjoyed when we finally, after numerous years of trying and against all odds, found out we were pregnant. It was unspeakably devastating for both of us when, only a few weeks later, a miscarriage again crushed our dreams of having a baby. At that point we decided it was time to start seriously looking into adoption.

Once the decision had been made, we had a renewed excitement as we began the process. We felt hopeful that we were finally on our way to getting a child. We filled out reams of forms, survived interview after interview, and completed the detailed home study. Finally, all there was left to do was wait, so we waited . . . and waited . . . and waited. After waiting for nearly five years, we had all but given up the hope of ever having a child of our own.

Now, only weeks after my confession of adultery and in the midst of the most frightening rebuilding challenge of our marriage, totally out of the blue we received the most exciting news. A social worker phoned to tell us that there was a darling little boy available for adoption and, if we were still interested, we could go pick him up at his foster family's home in the morning.

IF we were still interested? How could they even ask that? Of course, we were still interested! We'd been trying to adopt ever since we found out how unlikely it was that we would be able to have biological children and, after all those years of jumping through one hoop after another, we had honestly begun to believe that that door had closed for us as well. One unexpected phone call had changed everything. It was hard to even take it in. Tomorrow was the day we had dreamed of for so long—the day we were actually going to hold OUR child!

It was even more amazing that they had said that our soon-to-be-son was just five months old. Early in the adoption process the state agency had warned us not to expect a baby —they were too hard to get. Since we had continually been reminded that we would most likely be getting a bit older child, we didn't have a thing in the house for an infant—not a diaper, not a bottle, not a rattle—nothing. We were totally unprepared, but God took care of everything. Within hours, as our joyous news started to leak out into the community, people started stopping by our house with cribs and clothes and other baby things. We were in awe as we kept answering the door all afternoon to family, friends and people from the church bringing gifts for the little guy we were yet to see. Our house was absolutely crammed with baby gear by the time we headed to bed that night.

Even though we were exhausted from all the excitement, it was impossible to settle down. We were almost giddy with anticipation and hardly slept a wink all night. At 3:00 am we finally gave up and started out on the five-hour drive to meet our son. It felt like we were being given a whole new chance for happiness. Maybe the difficult times were finally behind us.

Becoming "instant" parents required a lot of new life adjustments—but it was great. I hardly had time to even think about sex. Those first few months with our little boy were wonderful for all of us. We loved him from the minute we first caught sight of his big blue eyes and chubby cheeks. He was big for his age and such a happy baby—he laughed all the time. The only time he ever got upset was if you didn't get food into his mouth soon enough when he was hungry.

Having a child and a new focus really brought Kathy and I closer together. The timing couldn't have been better—it was a real boost to our relationship. We absolutely dove into parenthood. Kathy took a few days off work at first, but since I was working swing shift, I had to quickly learn all the baby care skills like bathing, diapering and feeding so I could take care of our son during the day while she was working. It was a little scary, but I loved spending time with him and it was nice that our work schedules meant that we didn't have to put him in daycare or get a sitter.

NOW CHOOSE LIFE!

Since Kathy and I were on different shifts during the week, we especially cherished our weekends and the opportunity for the three of us to be together as a family. It was a magical time. Eventually, though, the newness of being a Dad started to wear off and I began to feel some of the old feelings and stresses again. In spite of my resolve and the joy that I had found in my expanded little family, I couldn't sustain my sexual sobriety long-term. I was just too screwed up inside.

Pornography began to creep back into my life. At first it was just once in a while, but it quickly gained momentum. It panicked me as I began to realize that, in many ways, I had become like a hardcore alcoholic that can drink and drink and never get drunk. My old coping skills just weren't working anymore. I used to feel calmer after I masturbated, but there were no positive feelings attached to it anymore. It didn't seem to resolve anything, or make me feel better. It just felt incredibly empty.

Ironically, the less it worked, the more time I spent at it. Sometimes I would masturbate so much in one day that my body would be totally depleted and I would climax without any semen. Still other times there would be blood. It scared me to death, but I kept desperately trying to make it work for me. I was frantic to get that calmness back. More and more, though, I found myself numbing out, getting depressed and sometimes even feeling suicidal.

As much as I adored our chubby little pre-schooler, and the sweet baby girl we added to the family a few years later, the rest of my life continued to slide downhill over the next few years. In the mid-'80s the company I worked for went on strike. When the employees refused to settle, the management just hired other laborers and left us out in the cold. After that, I was forced to take a bunch of low paying "survival jobs" like doing store inventories and stand-by custodial work. I felt pretty useless. Screwed up . . . ashamed ... useless—that's a trio that doesn't exactly build your self-esteem.

Eventually, I was able to find a full time job as a night janitor for a variety store. I hated working graveyard even more than I had disliked being on swing shift. It made everything worse. I was never home—never with my family. I usually tried to get up in the evening to have a little time with them before they went to bed, but after spending most of the day with pornography and very little time sleeping, I was so exhausted I could barely function. My depression got worse. The numbness got worse. Kathy assumed that I was in such bad shape because I hated my job so much, but there was a lot more to it than that. From time to time she'd catch me with some magazines and I'd go through the motions of throwing them away to get her off my back, but then I'd go out and buy new ones the next day. I think she knew, but we never talked about it. Nearly all my waking hours were now taken over with thinking about, buying, or looking at porn.

I tried hard to resist the lure of the massage parlors, and did for several years but, ultimately I lost the battle and started adding them to my repertoire once again. This time I told myself that as long as I didn't have intercourse, it wasn't so bad. Somehow I had myself pretty convinced that if I stuck to hand jobs it really wasn't adultery.

All this time I was still going to church and I was still living a "successful" double life. In spite of my actions, I sincerely loved God, but I was having a hard time believing that, with all my failures, he could still love me. I prayed regularly that He would take it all away and got extremely frustrated when it didn't happen. At one point, when I was praying, I plainly heard God tell me that I needed to talk to someone. But who in the world could you talk to about something like this? It didn't even seem like an option, so I tried to shove the idea out of my mind. My secrets kept me lonely and afraid. I was petrified all the time that I was going to be found out

Sometimes, when we're not really hearing what he's saying, God will use bizarre avenues to get our attention. One day an article in one of my porn magazines caught my eye. It was a satirical piece on sexual addiction. It talked about how some people thought that there was such a thing as sexual addicts—people that were so out of control that they couldn't get enough pornography and masturbation.

NOW CHOOSE LIFE!

In the article it listed the things that the "experts" saw as the signs of sexual addiction. The author was having a great time poking fun at each point, but as I read through the list I remember thinking "this is me—I have every one of these." According to the criteria in the article, I was, without a doubt, a sex addict. I finally had a name for my struggle.

Janet . . .

Not all inappropriate sexual behavior is indicative of sexual addiction. Having an affair or occasionally using pornography does not automatically classify someone as a sex addict. All non-marital sexual activity is, of course, outside of God's will and qualifies as sexual sin, but it is not necessarily addictive behavior.

Addiction specialists agree that certain factors must be present for a substance or behavior to be considered an addiction. These elements include:

> 1. COMPULSION - Addiction robs a person of their ability to make choices about their behavior and drives them to do the very things they have vowed not to do. Romans 7[3] talks about this desire to do one thing but being compelled to do another.

> 2. OBSESSION - Addicts eventually become so preoccupied with their addiction that they start to increasingly ignore work, family, hobbies, and other areas of their life, to focus solely on their addictive cycle. Bruce says he is not exaggerating when he says that it got to a point where he rarely thought about anything but sexual fantasies and how he was going to get more of them. When he got into recovery he was surprised how much room there was in his brain for other things.

3. PERSISTENCE - Persistence is the most undeniable sign that a person is addicted. Even when an addict faces dire, life damaging consequences because of their actions, they seem powerless to stop the behavior that is leading them toward that unwanted negative outcome.

4. TOLERANCE – As we mentioned in an earlier chapter, addictive behavior is also governed by the rule of diminishing returns. This means that as time goes by it takes more and more of a behavior or a riskier behavior to get the same "high" or feeling of relief.

If these indicators are present, it is very likely that you are dealing with an addiction. It is difficult, however, for most people to admit that they are no longer in control of their actions—that they are powerless to permanently stop their behaviors —that "addict" is a label that describes them. They desperately hang on to the hope that it is untrue and that there is another, less shameful, explanation.

It is equally challenging for many family members to comprehend that their loved one may have a struggle of this magnitude. It is not unusual for a man or woman to be shocked to discover that their spouse has been leading a secret life "under their nose" for years. Their partner's shame and the belief that the addiction is what helps them survive, has honed their ability to hide their behaviors —especially from those they are closest to.

Sexual addiction is one of the most misunderstood of all compulsions. Even many professionals do not fully understand the root and treatment of sexual addiction. The most difficult concept to grasp and remember, is that sexual addiction is not about sex. Whether we are aware of it or not, it actually represents a hunger for true intimacy with both the Creator and His creation.

The Bible says God created us to worship him alone, but in our ignorance or fear we often choose other earthly things to take that place of honor in our lives. If we have been abused or rejected at a young age, as so many addicts have been[4], it is especially difficult for us to trust people or even God. We become too afraid to seek the true intimacy that our heart desires and look, instead, for something that we hope will give us what we need without having to risk the pain that we are convinced would come if we really dared to open up to God and others.

If we discover that sexual activity numbs our fears and masks our internal pain, our brain tags it as being something that can make us feel "normal" again. When we experience pain or fear later on, our body remembers and starts to crave the very thing that diminished those feelings before. The more we choose that activity over running to God, the more ingrained it becomes. It quickly becomes our idol—the thing that we rely on to get us through the hard times. As it gains more and more place in our hearts, we increasingly move away from the source of life toward the death that addiction brings.

Addiction is unique in that it systematically destroys the whole person. Every aspect of our being (physical, mental, emotional, spiritual and social) is affected. As our acting out escalates, our thinking becomes increasingly distorted and the sexually compulsive rituals become a desperate substitute for our true needs for safety, acceptability and love.

No matter how much sex an addict gets, however, it is never enough to fill the void in their heart. Each encounter leaves them feeling even more empty and alone. They become separated from God, separated from family, cut off from those who would provide encouragement and support. This increasing isolation creates an environment that further erodes a person's mental, emotional and even physical well-being.

Only God can bring an end to the continual searching to be filled—everything else will eventually let us down.

Once established, addictions do not just go away by themselves. They won't disappear by ignoring them, denying them, or by relying on sheer willpower to stop them. Changing behaviors is not the same thing as true healing.

There are many popular therapy methods that promote behavioral change alone. All too often addicts that have had some success at "white knuckling" for a period of time mistakenly think that they have been healed using the techniques that have been offered

Unfortunately, in reality, they have only become one of two things—either a walking time bomb, ready to explode back into their addiction whenever the pressures of life break down their stubborn resolve not to act out, or an asexual being that finds a new compulsion like alcohol, drugs, gambling or work to numb them out and relieve their unwanted feelings. Without dealing with the core issues that caused the sexual addiction in the first place the addict will always need something to keep them from feeling the pain.

Even though an active addict may believe that they are somehow avoiding pain through their compulsive behaviors, they are, in actuality, only choosing a different kind of pain. An addict really only has two choices and both of them have negative consequences. They can continue acting out with the realization that using sex to meet their deep internal needs leads to increasingly destructive behavior. It will progressively damage their ability to function in personal relationships and grow spiritually in their relationship with God. Or, they can allow Jesus to help them face their painful memories, fears of rejection and sinful beliefs and free them from their grip. In Romans 6:14 Paul assures us "For sin shall not be your master, because you are not under law, but under grace." God wants to deliver us from addiction's grip, but he will not force us to accept his gift of "life more abundant." It is ours to choose or reject.

True change can only happen when the pain of the addiction becomes greater than the pain of changing.

12

The Denial That Ended Denial

Denying Christ on the Way to Surrender

Bruce . . .
The revelation that I was a sex addict made me feel even more hopeless than before. Having a "diagnosis" made the problem more tangible and insurmountable and took my depression to a new level.

Pornography hadn't been working for a long time and massage parlors had lost their excitement as well. I had never really cared for the fact that the women there held all the power and told you what they were going to do. But, in spite of that, I couldn't quite let go of them. I was still going from time to time, when several of the parlors got busted. People got arrested, names were printed in the newspaper and the places were closed down. I worried for a long time that my name would be found in the materials that were confiscated, but, thankfully, nothing ever came of it.

The busts brought an end to massage parlors in Whatcom County for a good long time. Once they were gone, I started thinking more seriously about prostitutes. I needed a step-up of adrenaline to counteract my growing depression and numbness, and I rationalized that I would have more control about what happened with a prostitute—which would certainly feel safer emotionally.

NOW CHOOSE LIFE!

I found a Canadian newspaper at the adult bookstore that advertised women that worked out of their homes and apartments. Since they were across the border and in private residences, the risk of being busted or caught seemed minimal. I called one and drove the half hour or so up to her place one day when I was supposed to be sleeping. Part of me couldn't believe I was stooping to this, but after each visit that horrible numbed-out feeling would leave for a little bit and the depression would lift. It was like shooting up a drug and feeling it take effect. Ah, yeah . . . there it is! Sometimes the high would last for a few days or even a week and then the numbness and depression would settle in again. But this new outlet did help make me feel better—at least for a little while.

It also scared me a bit, though. I wondered what would happen when this didn't do it for me anymore. Everything I had done in the past had eventually stopped working. What would I progress to next? I was already doing things that went completely against my value system—things I never thought I would do. I was just like a drug addict–except my body was creating its own drugs. I was painfully aware that it was only a matter of time before I would need something more.

I soon found out that "more" involved taking greater risks. Like the time I called a woman that was, unbelievably, advertising in our local daily paper. She offered to come over to my house and give me a massage and, like the massage parlors I had frequented before, she hinted that for tips there would be more. She promised that she would take her time. No rush. It sounded great and I told her to come on over.

She drove into our cul-de-sac, parked down the street and walked up to the door, in plain sight of any neighbors that might be watching. Then, while my wife was at work and the kids were at the babysitter, we "did it" right in the bed that Kathy and I had shared for over twelve years. Later I realized that it was the combination of the danger and the possibility of consequences that made it even more exciting . . . and more scary. That whole lifestyle is scary and I was in a constant state of fear. But, as time goes by, you actually start looking for the scarier path, because it ultimately brings a bigger high.

Many people, including myself, would look at my history of escalating sexual sin and wonder, first of all, how I could do the things I had been doing and still be a Christian, and second, how long it would be before God would get tired of my constant failures and reject me. As unbelievable as it seemed, no matter how bad my choices became, I constantly encountered a God who loved me and tried to draw me closer to him.

One night, while the rest of the household slept, I was awakened out of a deep sleep. I felt strongly that God was telling me to go out into the living room where I wouldn't disturb anyone, because he wanted to talk to me about something important. It's difficult to describe the experience. In ten years of being a Christian, this had never happened to me before. It wasn't like I heard a booming voice or anything, but I definitely felt compelled to go into the other room and I had no doubt, at the time, that it was a request from God.

As I settled into an overstuffed chair, the room was totally quiet. I sat in silence for a few minutes and then I felt God speaking again. He asked me "Bruce, Is your house more important to you than I am? Before I could even answer, he followed with another question, "Is your job more important than I am?" And then he asked even tougher questions: "Is your wife more important than I am? How about your children? Are your children more important than I am?"

I couldn't figure out why He was asking me these questions, but I answered as truthfully as I could. "Father, I don't know if I can say that you're number one, but I want you to be. Help me to make you number one."

He responded, "There is a very difficult time coming up when all those things will be in jeopardy and all you will have is me." I didn't know what he was talking about, but it felt like He was preparing me for something. It was mystical and mysterious and a bit frightening.

NOW CHOOSE LIFE!

I told Kathy the next morning and she thought it was kind of weird, as well. The conversation stayed with me, but nothing changed right away. In fact, it was over nine years before I truly understood what he had been telling me.

Soon after that encounter, I stopped going to church, altogether. I had always despised hypocrites and now I felt like I was being one. I didn't want to sit in church with one face and then look and act completely differently when I walked out the doors. I felt like Moses when he ran into the wilderness after he killed the Egyptian and hid out in his shame. I, too, was running because of shame. I wasn't hiding from God. I was hiding from people. I never lost my faith in God, I just didn't know how to be the "overcoming Christian" I knew people expected me to be.

By now, I was feeling totally numb most of the time. I couldn't feel happy. I couldn't feel sad. I couldn't feel depressed. I felt nothing. I knew there was something seriously wrong with someone who couldn't feel ANYTHING.

Feeling numb was worse than anything I had ever experienced before. I felt like the walking dead—a zombie. Hollow. Empty. I honestly felt more dead than alive most of the time and I started to toy with the idea of killing myself just to bring an end to the horrible numbness.

I cringe when I hear people joke that sexual addiction would be the "fun" addiction to have, when I so vividly remember sitting in my living room trying to decide which of my guns I should put into my mouth, knowing full well that I was ready to pull the trigger. I didn't want to live like this anymore and I was losing all hope of ever changing. I was exhausted, and I was becoming more and more accepting of the reality of death. If I just gave in and let it win, my struggle would be over and I could be at peace at last. I wouldn't have to fight off the terrible, awful enveloping cloud of death any longer.

There was a tiny little ember in me, though, that was still looking for a different solution for the dismal plight I was in. My quest led me to the streets of Vancouver, B.C. driving around the neighborhoods where I knew I would find prostitutes. I had never picked one up off the street before—that was the kind of thing you only saw in bad movies. But, this day I found myself pulling over to talk to one of them. When she came up to the window of the car I realized that she couldn't have been more than eleven years old. It repulsed me and I hurriedly drove off.

There was something exciting about the visual aspects of shopping for sex—some of the women had bizarre clothes, others really tight jeans or incredibly deep cleavage. The power was in my hands. I got to choose whatever struck my fancy. I was in control of the situation. I got to tell them what I wanted to do. I stopped and talked to a couple different women, but they all seemed to have an attitude that turned me off. Eventually, I settled on one with a really short skirt and fish net stockings. She looked slutty in a "healthy" way. Not too much make-up. Kind of pretty. A naughty girl-next-door type.

She quoted me her price, and when I agreed to it, she hopped into the car beside me. She told me she was a student working her way through school. I liked the idea that she wasn't just another drug addict trying to get money for her next fix. It made it seem more normal.

As we drove to the hotel she liked to use, she picked up a church bulletin that was sitting on the dashboard of the car. "Are you a Christian?" she asked. I knew if I said yes, I wouldn't be able to go through with it, so I said, "no, that's my wife's."

I felt a pang of conviction the minute I heard those words come out of my mouth, but I shoved those thoughts out of my head. The act of picking this woman up off the street had made me feel more alive than I had felt in a long time and I didn't want to lose that. It weirded me out that it was taking something like this to make me feel again, but by then we had pulled up in front of the raunchy-looking hotel she usually worked out of, so I pushed my guilt and self-condemnation away and followed her inside. It cost an extra $10 to *use her beat-up old room, but the only alternative was to do it in the car, and I couldn't bring myself to doing that.*

During the sex act, I noticed that she was dissociated most of the time. It made me really mad that she zoned out, looked around the room and didn't pay any attention to me. She was treating me like a nobody that didn't matter and that really pissed me off. My feelings were so intense they scared me. It was the first time I realized I had anger toward women. I worried that maybe I was in danger of turning into a rapist. When it was over, I drove her back to her street corner and left.

During the long drive home I felt really high. The highest of the highs . . . but, at the same time, the lowest of the lows. There was something wrong with me. How could I feel good about this? It was really bad. This was the kind of thing that really perverted people did. Not only was I willing to risk everything else—my family, my reputation, my self respect—but I was even willing to deny God to get a high.

Even though I felt better than I had felt in a long time, I decided on the way home that I had to get help, and if that didn't work, I was going to go through with shooting myself. Although it should have been obvious for a very long time, I finally realized that this wasn't something I could ever resolve by myself. I had no choice but to go talk to someone like God had told me to do so many years before

"Okay, God. You were right. I can't do this myself. I DO have to talk to someone, but I don't know who to talk to. Who DO you go to talk to about something like this?"

But, God didn't tell me that part . . .

Janet . . .

How does a sensitive little boy get to the point where he is so out of control in an addiction, that he can see no way out of his struggles but to take his own life?

How does a Christian with integrity and morals in every other area of his life end up in a seedy hotel with a prostitute?

How does a man who prays, reads his Bible and hears from the God of the universe get to a place where he is willing to deny his Lord and Savior?

How does a man who truly loves his wife and children more than he loves himself, risk them all for yet another fleeting high?

How do you reclaim and redeem a life that has been filled with so much hurt, confusion, denial and bad choices?

How do you start to let God restore what the locusts have eaten?

There are no answers until we first admit defeat.

Part Two:

Grasping for a Lifeline

*I called on your name, Lord, from
the depths of the pit. You heard my plea:
"Do not close your ears to my cry for relief."
You came near when I called you, and
you said, "Do not fear."*
                    Lamentations 3:55-57

13

OK, God . . .
but Who?

Starting to Reveal Lifelong Secrets

Bruce . . .
It, admittedly, took me a very long time, but I finally realized that I had no choice but to give in and do what God had asked me to do so many years ago.

I had proven over and over that I was not going to be able to stop my addictive behaviors alone. It was obvious that I DID need to talk to someone about my problem, just like He had said. But here I was—weeks after I had come to that conclusion—and I didn't feel a bit closer to following through with it than I had been on that long drive home from seeing the prostitute.

I knew I had to do it. I knew it was time, but I was so scared. I couldn't decide who to talk to and I couldn't figure out how to even start to bring up a topic like this. I rehearsed the conversation over and over in my mind, but nothing ever seemed quite right.

Even though I hadn't been to church in months, I finally decided that our pastor would be the best person to open up to. He had always seemed like a kind man—a fair man. I still didn't have a clue what I was going to say to him, but I went ahead and made the appointment anyway.

As the time got closer, my stomach began to twist itself into a knot. I kept wishing that there was another way. I didn't want to admit the shameful things I had done, but I desperately wanted off this runaway train.

I still struggled to find the right words as I spoke with him in his office. I tried, but I just couldn't bring myself to disclose everything—it didn't feel safe—so I told him that I had been very depressed and thought I needed help—like a counselor. Could he recommend one? It wasn't a lie—I was EXTREMELY depressed— but it certainly wasn't the whole truth, either.

I beat myself up all the way home for chickening out and not being completely honest, but at least I had gotten the name of a counselor. I had a place to start. At that moment I fully believed that I was on the home stretch now. I would go to see this counselor a few times, find the underlying problems in my life, fix them, and get this nightmare behind me, forever.

Unfortunately, it didn't work out quite the way I had it planned.

The counselor I had been referred to turned out to be a woman but, in spite of my confusion relating to most females, I felt reasonably comfortable with her right from the start. Other than feeling a little awkward, the first two sessions went very well. We talked about depression in general and the specifics of what I'd been experiencing. It was the first time I actually felt heard by someone. It was an amazing feeling.

On the third visit, however, Gwen sent me into a tailspin by saying "I don't see your depression as that big of a problem. I'm confident that in time, it will take care of itself. You're going to be fine. In fact, I can't even see any reason for you to keep coming to me."

Panic gripped me. I couldn't let her send me away. I still had so much that needed to be said. I didn't want to stop now. I finally just blurted out what I had never been able to tell anyone before. I told her about my sexual struggles and my inability to control them and their escalation. It was actually kind of relief to get it out in the open.

To my surprise, she didn't seem shocked or disgusted. She listened intently and then suggested that I read the book "Out of the Shadows[5]" before our next visit. I bought the book on the way home and devoured every page. It was such an eye-opener. I felt like I was reading an autobiography. The feelings and beliefs the author described were so familiar to me that it was almost like I'd been the one he'd interviewed for the book. By the time I had finished reading it I had absolutely no doubt that I was dealing with a sexual addiction problem.

When I returned for my next counseling appointment, I told Gwen what I'd read and what I had understood it to mean. She told me that I had a special gift—that not every one was able to read a book, decipher it, and glean things for their life like I could. Her affirming words made me feel good and gave me a new hope that maybe I could get past this.

A few weeks later she met with Kathy. She explained to her that I was struggling with a sexual addiction. She told her what that was and how I was actually unable to stop it by myself at this point—I would need help. She assured her that even though I was not yet capable of controlling my behavior, I had taken a huge and praiseworthy step in reaching out.

Although I'm sure it was extremely difficult information for my wife to hear, it undoubtedly explained a lot of what had been going on in our house for the past thirteen years.

I was deathly afraid that Kathy would be repulsed by what she learned and leave me, but instead I found her to be understanding and supportive right from the start. Even as I began to face the demons of the past and slipped deeper into the ugly pit of depression, she continued to stand by me.

In talking about my past, Gwen was the first one to tell me that what I had experienced growing up was not normal. The unpredictable rage, the emotional distancing, the attitudes toward sex, the inability to resolve issues, the secrets and silence —none of it was healthy —and in many cases it was abusive. I began to understand a little bit of how I had gotten so screwed up.

All in all, I saw Gwen for almost six months. It was a good start. I learned a lot about myself and my family but, if anything, it created even more reasons for me to act out. The deeper we delved into my past, the more it hurt and the more I wanted relief.

The only way I had ever known to deal with pain was by losing myself in pornography. It became almost routine for me to leave my counselor's office and walk directly to the adult theater, that was conveniently located across the street, to soothe my mind and emotions with more sexually arousing images

The more we talked, the more I acted out. I'm not sure if Gwen realized what I was doing or not, but she did understand that I needed a different kind of help than she could offer. She told me about a new therapist that had recently moved into the building. She said that this woman specialized in sexual issues like mine and suggested I make an appointment to see her.

It was scary to think about starting over with someone new, but I will always be grateful that Gwen realized it was time to push me out of the comfort of her nest so I could begin the next phase of my recovery.

Janet . . .

Because of an addict's intense fear of rejection, it is rare that their initial disclosure is the whole story. There are often many "false starts", just as Bruce encountered, before they are able to reveal the true nature of their struggle.

Although it is difficult to talk about any type of compulsive behavior, sexual issues still seem to carry a higher level of shame. Alcoholics or drug addicts that "come forward" are applauded. There is a level of acknowledgement and understanding concerning their struggle that helps to soften the pain of disclosure. Society tends to rally around them in support of their positive movement toward recovery.

Men or women that disclose a sexual addiction, however, are frequently labeled a pervert, slut, or sexual predator, even by their own family members. Stragglers are often afraid that if they share the exact nature of their issues they stand a good chance of being shunned, shamed or feared, like others that they have seen or known. Those apprehensions, whether justified or not, keep many people from seeking the help that they desperately need.

Even in the workplace the discovery of an alcohol problem is usually met with more compassion than the zero tolerance given to pornography use. Access to recovery programs for alcohol and drug abuse are often included in a company's benefit package. It is currently estimated that 25-40% of men and a fair number of women struggle with compulsive sexual behaviors. It is hoped that the growing awareness of this prevalence of sexual addiction will help to increase the acceptability and support of these recovery efforts, as well.

Bruce was lucky. His admissions were met with encouragement and support. The positive responses he received from both his counselor and his first wife made it possible for him to continue the difficult task of relinquishing his secrets and shame. Had his disclosure been met with name-calling and disgust, he may not have been able to find the courage to continue the recovery process.

While the situation required that Bruce take a direct approach when he finally admitted his problem to his counselor, it is not unusual for people to "test the water" by reporting instead of confessing. Talking about past struggles distances us from current behaviors and provides a form of insulation from negative reactions. If the disclosure of past offenses (whether truly in the past or not) gets a negative response, it shows the individual that it's not safe to share any more of their secret world.

Although it inherently carries a greater risk, a more direct and complete approach usually elicits more long-term positive support from loved ones than the progressive disclosure that re-wounds the hearer with each new admission. Spouses often express frustration when the story they get from their loved one comes in a series of small disclosures that erode trust and make them fearful of when the next "bomb" will be dropped in their lap.

Even when someone is fully committed to recovery and desires to "come clean", full disclosure may not initially be possible, because individuals very often discover additional memories or insights as their recovery progresses. These will come as God directs. This is different than the false assumption that it is somehow kinder to dole out the story a bit at a time. Many small bites are not always easier to swallow than a few larger ones.

If someone is unsure how their family will react to their struggle it may be wiser for them to reach out first to a counselor or other trusted person and let them help talk to their family in a factual and supportive way, as Bruce chose to do.

14

New Hope;
New Risks

God Brings Assurance and Helpers

Bruce...

The door had been opened a crack. I had fearfully shared some of my most shameful secrets and, much to my surprise, I hadn't been rejected—not by my wife nor by Gwen. It was an enormous relief, but it hadn't done much to stop my constant acting out.

Granted, I hadn't been back to the massage parlors since I first started my counseling sessions, and the only prostitutes I was seeing were the ones I played with in my fantasies, but I was frustrated that I could seldom make it through a day without masturbating with a pornographic magazine or movie.

I had a mixture of fear and new hope as I made an appointment with the therapist Gwen had referred me to. I was blown away at our first meeting when, without me saying a word, she pretty much described everything I'd been thinking and doing in recent years. I remember realizing "wow, this lady really knows what's going on. I'm not going to be able to pull the wool over HER eyes."

Even before we had a chance to talk, she seemed to know me and what made me tick far better than I knew myself. She knew about addiction and I would soon learn that she had that unique combination of toughness and compassion that you need to be an effective addiction counselor. She wasn't afraid to confront—but she also exuded understanding and encouragement as I struggled to work down to—and through—the source of my pain.

It was such a "God thing" that Emily even crossed my path. In talking with her I discovered she had a thriving practice working with court ordered sex offenders in Edmonds, Washington, a little over an hour away. About six months before our first meeting, she said she had been praying and felt that God had told her that she should open a satellite office in Bellingham. It gave me the chills when I realized that the timing of her prayer coincided almost exactly with the day I first "cried uncle" and asked God to send me someone who could help me climb out of the mess I had gotten myself into. He graciously provided Gwen to help me get started while Emily began the process of setting up a second office, but I have no doubt in my mind that Emily was God's answer to my heart-felt cry for help.

It's hard to appreciate today what an incredible miracle it was for me to find Emily. In 1988 the field of sexual addiction therapy was still in its infancy. Patrick Carnes had written his ground-breaking book "Out of the Shadows" just a few years earlier. Even though sexual compulsions had undoubtedly existed before that, hard-core pornography hadn't become widely available until the early 70's and, as near as I can tell, the term sexual addiction wasn't coined until the 80's. Still today there is a limited understanding about this addiction among many professionals, but back then it was almost non-existent. And yet, God brought one of the few specialists at the time practically to my doorstep.

At first Emily didn't push me to stop acting out. In fact, it took nearly a month just to complete all the psychological testing she had me do—mental health screenings, personality tests, chemical dependency assessments. She even insisted that I do a Plethysmograph test. She explained to me that the penile plethysmograph measures the blood flow to the penis in response to sexually suggestive photos, movies or audio. It's able to detect sexual arousal before a person is even aware of it themselves.

New Hope; New Risks

Since she said it was a requirement if I wanted to continue therapy with her, I scheduled the test. It was scary and embarrassing as the test facilitator hooked me up to the machine and told me what to expect. He said he would show me a variety of graphic pictures and the equipment would measure my response. There were pictures of scantily clad women in seductive poses, hookers, rape scenes, homosexual encounters, and little girls dressed to look much older and sexier than they should have been. Some of the photos disgusted me. Others were pleasurable.

When the test was over and the facilitator announced I was "normal" and was aroused by conventional sexual images and not by the photos depicting more deviant sexual behaviors, a wave of relief washed over me. Until then I hadn't allowed myself to even acknowledge how much I secretly feared that my fixation on sex and my escalating behaviors might indicate that I had the potential to become a sexual perpetrator of some sort.

Armed with the assurance that I was not a predator or sexual deviant, Emily and I began to go to work in earnest. She told me that my sexual addiction was just a symptom of some deeper issues. Although I didn't know it at the time, I realize now that over the next five or six months our discussions and homework led me through the 12-steps—the addiction recovery process used by Alcoholics Anonymous. When she got to what is commonly known as Step 5 (Admitting to God, to ourselves and to another human being the exact nature of our wrongs) she said it was time for me to go back and tell my pastor the truth about my struggle.

I was scared to death to attempt it again. I had chickened out so badly the first time. In spite of my positive experiences with Gwen, Emily and my wife, I was still convinced that if I told the whole story to anyone, I would be judged or misunderstood. I wrestled with myself and procrastinated for several weeks. During that whole time I was full of anxiety and could barely sleep at all.

Each week when I went to my counseling session, Emily would remind me of how important it was to share my struggle with someone else. The combination of her unrelenting prodding and my own internal angst eventually wore me down and I finally made arrangements to go see the pastor.

The conversation began kind of tenuously. I didn't quite know how to start so I asked him, "Do you remember a few years ago when I told you I was depressed?" I paused until he acknowledged that conversation. "Well, I went to see the counselor you suggested and after a few months she referred me on to someone who is more of an expert in what I'm struggling with—sexual addiction with pornography." I cautiously watched his face as I continued to speak about my struggle and the challenges of my recovery. Much to my surprise, he didn't act shocked or judgmental. In fact his eyes, and later his words, expressed compassion for what I had been going through. It felt like he truly, genuinely cared about me and my story and that felt amazing.

I had imagined a lot of different outcomes to this meeting, but I never dared dream I would receive the acceptance and encouragement that I found that day. As I stood up to leave I felt so much lighter and freer than when I had come in, less than an hour before.

The pastor also rose out of his seat to shake my hand. As I thanked him for the meeting he leaned in toward me a bit and said, in a slightly hushed tone, "I'm so glad we had this little talk, but I really think we should keep this just between us. Don't tell anyone else in the church—they're not ready to hear this."

His words of caution reawakened and fed my belief that I was uniquely sinful and no one could or would understand. In the split second it took for him to say those words all the good feelings drained out of my body and were replaced with new shame. I felt more alienated than ever from the people at the church.

Janet . . .

In today's society there is a heightened awareness of the prevalence of sexual predators in our communities. News programs, talk shows and magazines are increasing their efforts to educate their

New Hope; New Risks

audiences and get sexual predators off the streets. It is important that we continue to make our neighborhoods safer places for both ourselves and our children.

Unfortunately these efforts, that are intended to bring about positive change, are also causing damage to many, many people who are addicted to porn. Although it has been widely reported that the majority of rapists, sex offenders, and mass murderers have a history of pornography use, most sexual addicts have no predisposition to these more violent sexual behaviors. All too often there is no differentiation made between predatory sex offenders and those who are hiding from their pain with pornography.

Families, and even the sexual strugglers themselves, often worry needlessly that compulsive pornography use is an indication of a unique sinfulness or inherent flaw that makes them a danger to those around them. This is seldom the case. As Bruce found out through the Penile Plethysmograph, even as out of control as his addictive behaviors had become, he was still normal in what aroused him sexually. Pictures of children in sexual situations or rape scenes sickened him. He was a sensitive man who had simply stumbled upon an activity that, at first, was pleasurable enough to distract him from the intense feelings of unacceptability and the fear of rejection that had permeated his life from his youngest days.

We can't automatically assume that everyone who regularly drinks alcohol to excess will become a wino living in a cardboard box somewhere, nor should we assume that everyone who uses pornography or visits prostitutes is destined to become a sex offender. In our many years of working with men struggling to overcome sexual addiction, we have consistently found the majority of them to be the most sensitive and caring men we've ever met. It is often their sensitive nature and their desire not to hurt or be hurt that drove them to this particularly isolating addiction.

This does not mean that pornography is "no big deal." Although it may sound melodramatic, it can be every bit as damaging as a cancerous tumor or a bad heart. The disease of addiction will ultimately cost a person their life, whether literally or by simply commandeering their every waking moment. Experts tell us that

71% of addicts have considered suicide as the only hope for getting out of their addictive cycle. Many more addicts risk life-threatening disease through affairs and prostitutes. Allowed to flourish, sexual addiction ruins lives and systematically destroys both a person's self-esteem and their relationships with God and others.

Fear, shame and denial are the predominant reasons that people do not reach out for help. Once they realize that pornography has become more than just an enjoyable pastime and desperately desire to stop the escalating grip it has on their life, the attitudes they hear expressed around them frequently convince them that disclosing their struggle would put them in an even worse situation. So they try even harder to stop by themselves, fail miserably, beat themselves up, and stay stuck.

As Bruce found, there ARE people out there that will be supportive and helpful. God has brought many of them into his life throughout his recovery journey. But we, as a society and a Christian community need to consider whether our attitudes are making it harder for people to find the freedom that God desires for them.

Sexual addiction is more than just a sin issue. It IS sin—but no more or no less than anything else we use in place of God to keep us safe and make us feel normal. Sexual addiction is more than a lust problem. It is more than just "the way guys are made."

Sexual addiction has nothing to do with whether a person's spouse is attractive enough or "available" enough. It has nothing to do with being perverted or oversexed. In fact, as we discussed before —it is not even about sex, at all. It is about "zoning out", feeling adequate and decreasing internal agitation and fear. It is about not being able to trust or get truly close to people. It is about not feeling acceptable. It is about not being able or willing to feel or process our real emotions.

Only love, acceptance and grace can provide a safe enough environment for someone to look at and allow the very real issues behind their struggle to be healed.

15

Stopping the Engine

Preparing to Look at Deeper Problems

Bruce . . .
During the first few months with Emily I'd stop acting out for a day or two and then I'd be right back at it again. As counseling progressed, though, I began to take in the idea that I was using my acting out to numb the pain of some deep wounds from my past. With Emily's help, I realized that those wounds could never be ministered to and healed unless I would allow myself to feel and acknowledge the damage that had been done. I needed to get in touch with my hurts and my emotions and I couldn't do that as long as I was avoiding and numbing them with fantasies and pornography.

At first the best I could do to control my destructive behavior was just to try to stay away from the pornography. I would drive miles out of my way to avoid going near any stores that had magazines or videos. I would white-knuckle my way home from errands so I wouldn't stop at an x-rated theater. I would cloister myself in the bedroom to avoid a steamy movie, or a titillating documentary that was on TV. I felt so weak. I wanted so badly to be able to just say no and have that be the end of it. But, no matter how hard I tried to steer clear of temptation, I couldn't get away from my mind. All I could think about was sex, sex, sex. I would fantasize about going to bed with every girl I saw whether I was at the grocery store, at work, watching TV or even in church. I felt like there were two people with opposite poles struggling against each other inside of me and I would get so exhausted and depressed from the constant battle that I just wanted to lie down and bawl. Tears that had long since been shut off because "boys don't cry," threatened to spill over at any time.

There were other days I felt optimistic. I felt like there was hope. My mind would be refreshingly free from sexual fantasies. I would start feeling closer to Kathy and the kids. Then something would happen. . . a bad day at work . . . a disapproving comment . . . a phone call from my parents. . .a mistake. . .an inability to do something I thought I should be able to do . . . and I'd be back in the battle again. Any one of these things had the power to trigger my cravings to run away, act out and get lost all over again.

Still other times when I thought things were going well, I would unexpectedly stumble upon a magazine that I had long since hidden and forgotten, or find a letter in our mailbox from one of the phone sex services I had used. Every time I caught sight of one of these reminders I would want to open it so badly it almost hurt. Even if I gave it to Kathy or threw it away, my mind would keep wandering back to what might be in it. I knew there would be pictures of hot sexy women and detailed accounts of their fantasies. I also knew where "a quick peek" would take me and I didn't want to go there. . . but then that persistent addictive part of me would question whether just one more time would really be all that bad. In an instant, my mind would be off and running, all over again. It's a terrible thing to have something consume you so totally.

At one point Emily suggested that I might find added support and encouragement by attending Sexaholics Anonymous. Like before, the idea of sharing my struggle with someone new was terrorizing. It took me several weeks of procrastination before I could even get up the courage to call for more information

After I'd made the phone call, my anxiety continued to grow as the date of my first meeting drew closer. I was so worried that

I wouldn't fit in—that I would be somehow different than all the others— but when I finally got there I discovered that my fears were completely unfounded. The group was small—just three men—but it felt comfortable right from the start. I heard the other men expressing the same fears, doubts, anxieties, lack of worth and shame that I felt. It was like hearing my story come out of their mouths. When I shared my struggles I could see MY pain reflected in their eyes, but I was relieved to also see understanding and acceptance.

As difficult as it was to make myself go to the SAA meetings, especially if I was feeling tired, depressed or ashamed that my week had been less than victorious, I was always glad when I did. Over time our group grew in numbers and developed a special bond as we shared our struggles and successes with each other. It was amazing to realize that many of the things I felt the most ashamed about, were things that were common to the other men as well. The more I discovered that I was not uniquely flawed—not a freak—the more my paralyzing shame was reduced, and the more freedom and motivation I found to explore my own wounds and reach out to others for help during the crazy craving times.

All my efforts to avoid temptation and reach out for support were certainly helping. I was no longer acting out or thinking about acting out every waking moment, but after four or five months of grueling effort it was still a daily battle to keep from slipping back into old patterns. I continued to lose the battle more days than I won and I was starting to believe that I would never be able to control this monster.

Sensing my growing frustration, Emily told me about a drug called Depo-Provera that could help take away the cravings. It was the same drug they used for chemical castration and would reduce my interest in sex to almost nothing. She said that I would need to talk with Kathy and decide together if it was something I wanted to try.

Kathy, of course, wasn't exactly ecstatic about the prospect of a sexless marriage. She read the materials Emily had sent home and warily suggested that maybe we should go ahead and find out about the cost and whether our insurance would cover it. She also warned me that she wasn't sure whether it was something she was ready for or not.

The next couple of weeks, however, were a particularly rough period for me. The slide started on Saturday when I went and bought two pornographic magazines while everyone was out of the house. I came home and spent 4 solid hours looking at those magazines, calling phone sex numbers, and masturbating. I was exhausted by the time Kathy got home from work and she was livid because somehow she could tell I'd been acting out again. I still don't know how she could figure it out, but she usually had some kind of sixth sense about it and she was seldom wrong. I knew I had hurt her yet again, and I left for work angry at myself, depressed and tired of repeating the same old story.

Most of the rest of the week the pendulum swung wildly between frantic acting out —sometimes so much that my penis would be raw and sore—and simply fantasizing about sex all the time and sexualizing every woman that I saw. Even when I was able to stay away from the porn I felt like I was on the verge of acting out all the time. The constant fight made me tired and irritable with my wife, kids and co-workers.

The binge finally came to an end the following Friday when I stopped and rented two X-rated movies on my way home from running errands. I arrived back at the house about 10:30 that morning and spent the next three hours masturbating. My sister-in-law had been watching the kids and decided to bring them home about 1:30 assuming that I would be back from my errands by then. I managed to zip up and turn off the movie before they got in the house, but it was pretty obvious what I'd been doing. She knew all about my problem and told Kathy that afternoon what I'd been up to. Later, when Kathy and I talked about it, I was still reeling from how close the kids had come to catching me themselves. We agreed that I was going to need more help if I was every going to get a handle on this and decided we had no choice but to try the Depo-Provera. I *immediately made an appointment to have my first shot the following Monday.*

Even though Sunday night was usually my night off from my building maintenance job, I had to go to work that week because some big wig was coming up from Portland. My supervisor told me that I needed to strip and wax the whole variety end of the store. It was a huge section of floor and I was upset and angry. I knew I couldn't get it done in one night. I started looking at how much I had to do and it felt hopeless. But after I got going I concentrated on one aisle at a time. I just kept going and going and by 5:30 the next morning - I had one little section left to go. I looked back at how far I had come and I felt the Lord tell me, "see, I will give you just enough strength for one aisle at a time. Stop looking at the whole store or "mountain of your problem." I instantly realized that that was exactly what I had been doing. I had allowed myself to become totally overwhelmed by the enormity of my issues, when I really needed to be focusing on taking just one small step at a time.

Monday was a much better day. With the help of the Depo-Provera and the new realization that I couldn't change my whole problem at once—it was too big for me to handle—I began a new phase of my recovery. The shots really did help me control my fantasies and my behavior. I recommitted myself to moving forward one step at a time with God's help and Emily's tools. I accepted the fact that it was going to take a lot of work and time to get where I want to be.

Janet . . .

Mechanics know that there are only a few things that you can fix while a motor is actually running. You might be able to set the timing or adjust the valves, but more significant repairs require the engine to be stopped or even disassembled. The same is true with addiction. The repetitive out of control spinning of addictive thinking and behaviors prevents a person from being able to really look at the broken parts within them.

NOW CHOOSE LIFE!

Many people naively think that purposing in one's heart is all it takes to stop unwanted behaviors. They believe that if someone is really serious about changing, they just need to say no, use a little willpower, and never look back. People who struggle with any addiction, however, are well aware that it is much more complicated than that. Everything in them may detest what they are doing; they may want to stop so badly that they contemplate suicide as a means to do so, and yet they may still have tremendous difficulty distancing themselves from behaviors that, through years of repetition, have become as involuntary as sneezing.

It took the help of an experienced addiction counselor and a combination of different tools for Bruce to "stop the engine" so he could begin to look at the underlying causes for his automatic addictive responses.

Undoing anything that has become a habit, no matter how small, is an uphill challenge. Stopping habitual behaviors that are associated with self-protection and alleviation of lifelong pain can be agonizingly difficult. Desiring to stop does not automatically give a person new ways to deal with old triggers. If something painful, like the fear of abandonment, has always been suppressed by sexual activity, not running to that behavior opens the door for the full impact of those feelings to hit. Initially this onslaught of emotions can be so intense and overwhelming that it feels like a matter of life or death. Until some of the deep wounds have been healed and new ways to cope with the pain and fears have been learned, the person's whole being cries out for relief. It is not unusual for someone to even have actual physical withdrawal symptoms similar to those experienced by people coming off drugs.

In early recovery, successful attempts to avoid acting out can best be compared to getting a root canal with no anesthetic. It can be agonizing. Taking a stance of zero tolerance for slips at this point is an unreasonable standard that invites a return to secrecy and hiding. These setbacks, if handled correctly, can actually provide significant insight into the core beliefs that have, in the past, been triggers for the now unwanted behavior.

Usually one recovery method is not enough to sustain someone trying to overcome addiction. Even the Depo-Provera, which helped Bruce immensely, was not always enough to circumvent the intense cravings for his old behaviors. The following entry in Bruce's journal about nine months into recovery illustrates how difficult the stopping process can be, as old pain is allowed out in the open:

> *HELP! I am having a bad time today. I want to act out so much. It is the worst impulse since I started Depo-Provera. I'm not sure why, but I am past the aversion therapy in the cycle. I white knuckled myself home today. I wanted to go to the bookstore so bad. I'm trying to figure out what triggered such a swing. Yesterday I got very emotional writing about my anger toward my mom and how I used that anger against prostitutes. I think I was trying to force myself into denial but it is hard to deny what you know is there. I realize now that I was allowing myself to go into a fantasy longer than I usually do before using aversion. I found myself wanting to stay there and hide! Reality is hard for me to deal with sometimes and I know I use acting out to get away from it. I wish I could call one of the guys from SAA, but they are all at work.*

Depo-Provera was just one component in Bruce's recovery efforts. He also mentioned using aversion therapy, willpower, journaling and group support. All of these can be extremely helpful tools—but as we see from his writing, even all those precautions were sometimes insufficient to eliminate his cravings for old relief measures.

Practical thought stopping exercises, often called Aversion Therapy, can be extremely helpful in the early stages of recovery. Some therapists suggest that wearing a rubber band that can be snapped, pinching oneself, or loudly yelling NO! or STOP! can help startle someone out of the automatic thinking patterns of addiction.

Bruce had some success with these methods when thoughts and fantasies would begin to churn in his mind. When he found himself lingering on a television program with suggestive content, wanting to stop and buy a magazine on his way home, or fantasizing about a prostitute he had encountered, a sharp snap from the rubber band he wore would help him detach from the images and often allowed him the opportunity to make the decision to move away from the addictive cycle.

He also found support and encouragement in the SAA group he was attending. In addition to reducing his shame, these men also provided a lifeline for Bruce. Often just being able to talk about a struggle with someone who truly understands, helps to reduce the power of the cravings. Regularly meeting with others who share that same struggle, especially if some of them have achieved a measure of success in their recovery, has been scientifically shown to increase a person's serotonin level which reduces agitation and helps them relax, feel at peace, and gain hope.

Recovery is a process. Ups and downs, good days and bad days are normal for an extended period of time for most recovering addicts. It is only with unrelenting perseverance and God's help that abstinence and healing begin to gain momentum.

16

War of the Minds

Learning to Feel Real Emotions and Recognize Truth

Bruce . . .
The whole time I was seeing Emily, she insisted I keep a journal. Every day I would write about the things that I was experiencing. Some of my writing just documented the daily activities of my family, but I also wrote about my thoughts, emotions, struggles, victories, fears, the things we were discussing in my counseling sessions, and even what I dreamed about at night.

At first it felt strange to be putting such personal information down in black and white, but it quickly became a safe place to process things between our sessions and record the issues I still needed help in working through. As I was nearing the end of the first year of my counseling with Emily, my journal entries clearly reflected the roller coaster of new emotions I was experiencing—the very emotions I had strived so hard to avoid in the past and could barely accept, let alone resolve.

> *Wednesday—November 9th*
> *I'm having a rough 24-hour period. I'm not really fantasizing about acting out, but I feel anxiety. The way I always handled anxiety in the past was to*

run to my addiction, so I know I could go there very easily and that causes even more anxiety. The worst part is that I'm not sure where the anxiety is coming from. Maybe it's because I'm alone today and that's when I'm usually at the highest danger.

Wednesday—November 16th
I'm going to the doctor this morning. I'm nervous and scared about talking to him about testing me for AIDS, but it's something that I, as a responsible man, must face for my own peace of mind and for the sake of those I love. Sometimes I'm still overwhelmed by the mess I've gotten myself into. The chances are slim that I came in contact with AIDS, but the possibility is a reality. God, help me take this one step at a time and not worry until it is time to worry.

Saturday— November 19th
On the way home from working graveyard this morning, I started thinking about stopping by the store and buying a magazine. I snapped my rubber band and yelled "stop!" I drove the long way around on the freeway to avoid going near the store and when I got home I fried up some potatoes the way I like them, poured a glass of milk and ate breakfast instead. I feel good about myself and my choices.

Monday—November 21st
I'm starting to feel positive about my recovery and my self-esteem is up even though I had a new attack from "my monster" last night. I had a dream that I was going into a store that looked like a general store from the outside. I walked in and it was an x-rated

bookstore. I started looking at all the material and got really turned on. A woman was running the store and that excited me even more. I woke up with an erection and was so turned on by the fantasy in the dream that I wanted to masturbate. I resisted temptation and white-knuckled myself back to sleep.

Tuesday—November 29th
I am so relieved to find out I am free of AIDS. I told Kathy and it took her by surprise. She was quiet for a while. When I asked her if she was all right she said she was shook up by the possibility of what could have been. She asked me if there were any more surprises down the road. I told her I couldn't think of any.

Saturday—December 3rd
I was so afraid to face the anger inside of me yesterday, but when I let go and just let it flow out of me, I was surprised that it was not anger that came out. I experienced much pain, fear, frustration, shame and emptiness, but no anger. It was coming out of me in waves and I sobbed and sobbed. After I was done and completely wiped out, I had no more urge to act out. It was the first time I escaped out the door in the acting out part of the addictive cycle. You'd think I would feel good, but I'm sad and completely empty now. I guess I just need some time to heal.

Sunday—December 4th
Today in our adult Sunday School class we studied the prophet Jeremiah. We learned how he prophesied the tearing down and rooting out of the old in order to build the new. It hit me that that's where I am.

Maybe I feel so empty right now because the old inner core belief system is being destroyed within me. I think Friday was some major demolition and I'm not sure how to rebuild in the vacuum that is left.

Monday —December 5th
One minute I feel empty and the next I'm crying and don't know why. Sometimes I wonder if I'm losing it. I had trouble today with fantasizing about some women I saw while shopping. I used aversion techniques after enjoying the fantasy for a while. I'm finding that I'm more and more distracted, lately. I'm afraid I'm building up towards another turn in the cycle. I got my shot but I feel like I'm on edge and it wouldn't take much for me to lose control. It really makes me realize how much I used my acting out to hide from everything from the smallest amount of stress to the larger difficulties of my childhood.

Wednesday—December 14th
I read some of my journal entries from September and October yesterday and I was reminded of how possessed I was with my fantasies. I don't want to go back to that. It scares me that it might come back after I am done with my shots. I hope my therapy will go far enough that it won't return or if it does I'll be strong enough to stop it.

Monday—December 19th
Kathy and I had another talk last night about our life and how we have changed. She says she feels like our sex life is so mechanical with no feelings. She is hurt that I do not include her in my fantasies. I feel guilty about that.

We made love last night but I could not maintain an erection without fantasies of prostitutes and swingers.

Thursday—December 22nd
I acted out yesterday!! I was confused to why. I thought about it all day. I checked back on things that happened to me in the last week and realized I was hiding from unpleasant feelings again. I feel guilty and inadequate in my sex life with my wife. I am upset and depressed about my family and Christmas. My sister hung up the phone on me because we weren't doing what she wanted. My Mom and Dad aren't coming for Christmas because Mom fell down and is sore.

I'm tired of having a fractured family and that brings out all those old feelings from my childhood. I feel like a clutz because I can't fix my cars and need to spend money on labor. I'm upset that I can't even read books that I would enjoy for fear that I'm going to read something that turns me on. All of these things contributed to my slip.

I acted out with a prostitute fantasy and I had a strong orgasm! But I was confused about not feeling any anger. Then I realized that my controlling the other person is a subtle act of anger. In my fantasy the person does what I want, so there is no noticeable anger. But with a real live woman (prostitute) they react to my attempts to control. Either they act bored and just want it over with which makes me MAD! Or they try to be friendly and be a real person which makes me MAD! again.

So, I do use my anger in sex whether through control in a subtle way or outright anger at someone for messing up my control by being a real person. God, I don't like my actions and feelings in regards to how I treat other people. And I'm still trying to hide from my feelings and reality. At least I am aware of it and I realize that it will take time to change a lifetime of messed up thinking. God's timetable is not ours.

Wednesday—December 28
I need to practice dealing with my feelings. I seem to be all right until something is painful or hurts and then I go on automatic shutdown. I know this is dangerous for me, so I will continue working on it.

Thursday—December 29
I'm on guard for my compulsion today. For the last 24 hours I've been thinking about my old swinger magazines and wondering if there are any new ads that I might be missing. I've thought about past visits to massage parlors. I find myself wanting to stay with the thoughts and fantasies. I have used aversion methods but I have allowed myself more time with the thoughts than I should. I've been having trouble dealing with my anger this week. I'm sure it is related. I've been laying in bed for the last 3-1/2 hours trying to go to sleep but fantasies of some of the prostitutes I have been involved with keep coming back and bothering me. I want to act on them! I even started to masturbate. I know I need to call someone but I don't want to. I've been telling myself I can handle it if I can just get to sleep— but my mind is too active and anxious . . .

Later that night . . .
I just called Charles and talked for 20 minutes. He's good for me. We are similar in our anxieties and thoughts and feelings. He gave me some more tools to work. It took all the will power I could muster to call him. I didn't want to do it. I wanted to handle it myself, but I was losing and I knew it.

Saturday—December 31
I did some thinking last night at work about my mom and I guess she was more rigid than I was remembering when I was talking to Emily yesterday. During our conversation I was thinking only of her inconsistency in discipline. But now I'm remembering that if Mom wanted something from us or Dad she could make life very miserable for everyone until she got it. I can see now that I really didn't have a very good role model for a mom or wife or for the female gender in general. I am beginning to appreciate how complex the human mind is, because this anger and my addiction is becoming more and more complex all the time. How Emily makes sense out of it, I'll never know. It also makes me realize why it takes so much time to change. Have a Happy New Year, Emily. May it be a quieter and brighter new beginning for us all.

Janet . . .

All too often pastors, spouses and other accountability people in the life of someone who has admitted to, or been caught in, a sexual compulsion expect instant transformation. Nothing but a clean cut from the old thoughts and behaviors is acceptable.

Only in the rarest of cases is healing from sexual addiction that instantaneous. In fact, it is frequently considered one of the most difficult addictions to overcome. More often than not it is an uphill battle that requires immense courage, stamina and prayer. Unless God is allowed to heal the deep-rooted causes of the addiction, the recovery rate achieved by traditional therapy has often been estimated at as low as 3%.

The more success Bruce had in controlling his behavior, the more anxious, scared and angry he became and the more desperately he hungered for relief. It was a constant battle. There were many days that everything in him wanted to just give in, buy a magazine and hide. And all too often, when he was feeling particularly weak, stressed or tired, he did just that—which would cause him to start hating himself all over again. Now with his new awarenesses, however, the old familiar self-loathing was also mixed with an intense anger that he had gotten himself into such an awful mess in the first place.

Zero tolerance for the old behaviors would have served little purpose other than to create more shame and secrecy—both of which work against the healing process. In our years of working with those struggling with sexual addiction, we've seen many sad situations where the disparity between the expectations of those around them and the addict's ability to immediately achieve that level of success has driven them into an even more ominous Jekyll and Hyde lifestyle. Instead of moving ever closer to freedom, they have become even more skilled at covering up their behavior and even more convinced that they are too sinful or too damaged to change. To the outside world they may give the appearance that they've been victorious. They learn to say the right things. Some even divert scrutiny from themselves by "preaching" abstinence to those who still struggle. They establish themselves as experts, when all the while they are more trapped than ever by their double life.

Unraveling the underlying causes of an addiction is often a long and difficult process. It is only the determination to keep plugging along and not give up that leads to longer and longer time between acting out episodes and eventually to an addiction-free life. Healing

War of the Minds

is a process, not an event. And, as with any process, problems will arise. Perfection will not always be achieved, but little by little new understanding and new skills will be acquired and the successes will begin to overshadow the struggles.

Nearly a year and a half after Bruce first sought help, he was still riding the roller coaster that is recovery as he learned first to acknowledge truths and feelings that he had been trying to ignore for his entire life and then, even more challenging, to figure out what to do with them. Having little or no experience recognizing and resolving anger, or feeling acceptable or powerful, he was often clueless at even knowing where to start. Some days he felt good about his choices and behaviors, other days he felt weighed down by depression or anger or shame. There were days he just didn't feel like fighting the fight and a part of him didn't even care if he won the battle or not. No matter if it was a "good" day or a "bad" day, every day was a kaleidoscope of swirling thoughts and feelings.

It is important, at this point in the process, to stay focused on the big picture and the forward movement—no matter how slight.

Addiction recovery is unknown and uncomfortable territory for most people and their families. When faced with this unfamiliar terrain, there is a strong natural desire to find some solid ground to stand on. In an effort to expedite that, the tendency is to continually try to extrapolate what the future is going to look like based on the current situation. A funny look or a cloud of depression may send family members into the fear that their loved one has given up and that all is lost. On the flip side, a positive attitude and a few good choices may be viewed as a sign that the battle is over and everything is going to be fine.

Since emotions and responses often change from day-to-day and minute-to-minute at this stage in recovery, trying to foretell the future by looking at any given moment is crazy-making. Even two years after Bruce first started counseling, his journal still reflected evidence of these erratic ups and downs. The swing was becoming increasingly less pronounced, but the pendulum had not yet come to a stop—nor were all the struggles behind him.

Sunday—May 7th
It's funny how life can look so different in just 24 hours. Yesterday I was angry and my trust of people was down and I was scared. Today I have new hope and believe in people more and generally feel upbeat.

Once realistic expectations have been established that provide room for the process, slips and struggles can become extremely valuable tools for growth and healing. Instead of recovery being temporarily derailed by the shame or frustration of a slip, that same event can be examined for whatever clues it holds about issues that still need healing. A glimpse of that process is shown in Bruce's December 22nd journal entry. He had come far enough in his recovery that instead of spending days kicking himself for failing, he voraciously began to analyze what had been going on in his life, what he was feeling and what false beliefs and authentic needs played into his actions. He discovered important information that was yet another piece of the puzzle that would, ultimately, free him from the grip of addiction.

One by one, little by little, God brought Bruce face to face with the many facets of his most painful wounds: the dysfunction of his family of origin, the fear that he wasn't a "normal" or "good enough" man, the confusion and anger he had about women and his own sexuality, and his intense fear of abandonment and feelings of powerlessness. Every new issue brought a rush of emotions, fears, and resistance, but he kept turning toward God for the strength and courage he needed to continue his healing journey.

Bruce found that God even used his dreams to help him work through difficult issues and to show him his progress. Early in his recovery his dreams were always about being faced with temptation and failing, but as he came to terms with some of his core struggles he began to internalize his recovery and make good choices and resolve conflict even in his dreams.

By being willing to experience the deep pain of past wounds and, with God's help and a lot of patience, work through them, change happens. It no longer requires trying harder or learning better techniques to do and feel the right things. Right and better feelings and actions spring naturally out of a heart that is being authentically and permanently restored.

> *Tuesday—May 9th*
> *I talked to Kathy about our sex life last night. I told her how I am beginning to experience love and emotions with sex for the first time in my life and it is so nice and beautiful compared to the loneliness and isolation of the sex I had the rest of my life. Kathy said that was always the hardest part for her. She knew I was not really there with her when we had sex in the past.*
>
> *The path is not always straight and consistent. Sometimes it feels like we have taken three steps forward and two steps back, but as we persevere we find that we didn't really lose ground, we only stepped back to get a better footing for the next leg of our healing journey. We will continue to experience the ups and downs, but as long as we're turning toward Jesus, we will never lose our way.*
>
> *Wednesday—June 7th*
> *I feel like I have gone backwards in my recovery. For a time I was becoming more loving towards Kathy. We were touching and communicating. Our sex life was getting better. Since I have started dealing with the anger I have withdrawn away again. I don't feel safe in touching or being touched. I'm not interested in sex and I don't cuddle and help Kathy. I think the fear of abandonment is really coming out in my anger. I'm not able to talk to Kathy as well as I was. I feel frustrated and my feelings are so unpredictable. It makes me wish I could go back to the hurting stage where I was in need of love. I think*

I need to direct my anger at the cause, but I'm not sure how to do it.

I feel frustrated over all this and a part of me feels like I want to shut down and go numb. It is a very hard time for me and for Kathy, too. This is the most difficult phase of healing I have come against so far. It must be tapping a deep-rooted hurt and anger that is very hard to face. I watched a show this morning on TV about adults that were physically abandoned by their mothers. It was extremely painful for me to watch. It reminded me of a quote I read once, I don't remember where—"Life begins as a quest of the child for the man and ends as a journey by the man to rediscover the child.[6]"

17

And Then There Were Three . . .

The Necessity of Letting Go to Move Forward

Bruce . . .

In spite of the many ups and downs I experienced in my recovery, there were days that I was absolutely overwhelmed by God's blessings and provision:

> *Sunday— January 1st*
> *Before I went to bed I prayed. I started thanking God for all the people who know about my problem and are still standing behind me. I was amazed and humbled by it. I told God how grateful I was for these loving people. My addiction was much too powerful for me to handle alone and without His help and all these people's help I would be lost. Tears started streaming down my face, I was in such awe of the power of God!*

At the time I wrote that journal entry, I didn't realize that there would soon be others joining me in my journey and some of my most trusted travel mates—like Emily—would unexpectedly begin to fade out of my life.

Less than two years after starting my counseling with her, Emily called me at home one evening to let me know that she would be closing her practice in Bellingham at the end of the year. Her startling announcement sent me into a panic. I credited Emily with quite literally saving my life and now she was telling me she was going away. Even though a part of me had always known that my time with her would eventually end, I never dreamed it would come so quickly or so abruptly. Everything in me wanted to find a way to talk her into staying. I was petrified that I wouldn't be able to make it without her. I wasn't ready for her to go.

The old voices in my head reawakened and began to tell me that I was being abandoned yet again. I agonized about whether I had done something to make Emily mad at me. I felt myself withdrawing from other people and having a hard time wanting to do anything. I became depressed and anxious. Even though I knew I was overreacting, I couldn't shake the old fears and feelings of rejection that enveloped me. It felt like everything I had worked so hard for was crashing down around me.

Emily reminded me in one of our remaining sessions that we can't move forward without letting go of the past—including old dependencies. It was time to let go of her hand and try using the tools she had taught me. Even though my stomach was still in a knot at the thought of not talking with her every week, I began to sense that God might have a purpose for closing this door.

Although I didn't know it then, God would allow me to continue seeing Emily off and on for the coming year at her Edmonds office. Cutting off our relationship didn't end up being as "cold turkey" as it originally appeared it was going to be, but it was still an extremely difficult separation. Emily had guided me through some really challenging times and helped me start to understand so much about why I was the way I was.

Eventually the end did come. And, in spite of the extra time I had been given to wean myself away, it was still terrifying. In those three years I had come to rely heavily on Emily to help me over the speed bumps that I encountered. I had to grieve the loss of my trusted counselor in the same way someone might grieve the death of a close family member. And, even when I was finally able to accept the fact that she would no longer be an active part of my life, I really wasn't sure how I was going to continue on in my recovery without her.

Emily explained to me that we had gone as far as we could with the addiction—her area of expertise—and that I needed a different form of counseling now. She referred me to a colleague, Karolyn, who specialized in dealing with abuse, family and spiritual issues. Emily believed that she was the one I needed to help me go deeper into the pain and hurt that I had uncovered in our sessions.

So . . . yet another counselor—my third—became a pivotal part of my recovery. It felt almost overwhelming to be starting over with someone new. Emily had grown to know me and my struggles so well. She often seemed to know me better than I knew myself. Now that history together was gone, and I had to make myself known to someone else. It was a tough time for me, but it was also a time that ultimately brought me to a place of new freedom and peace.

Karolyn helped me to really get in touch with some of the emotions and memories that I had been too afraid to look at before. More than just helping me remember things, though, she helped me work THROUGH the things I found. She utilized practices like hypnotherapy, healing prayer and EMDR[7], a psychotherapeutic tool for processing traumatic or distressing memories, to help me get in touch with and process the strong feelings and hurt that I had been carrying just under the surface for so many years.

Together we found and let God heal many of the wounds that had caused me to be vulnerable to addictive behaviors in the first place. It was a difficult and emotional period, but Emily was right, Karolyn's type of counseling was perfect for what I was experiencing (and needing to experience) at the time.

Karolyn also encouraged me to share what I had experienced with others. From time to time she would ask me talk with a man that was just starting recovery for sexual addiction and fairly early in our time together, she invited Kathy and I to go with her and another counselor to share our testimony to a group of nearly 100 Christian counselors. Kathy and I took turns talking about our experiences with sexual addiction and codependency. I was very nervous about the idea of speaking in front of a group, but especially about talking about something as personal as my addiction. As I started to talk, the words just flowed out of me. I only used my notes to get started. I'm not a natural speaker and I usually go blank in front of people, but God answered my prayer and gave me the words to say, as I needed them. Kathy and I both felt such a peace after we finished talking. We couldn't believe how many people came up and thanked us for our courage to share. It felt like we were doing God's will and He had been there with us.

For some time I had been fascinated by the whole recovery process and the counselor/counselee relationship. I had been continually amazed that Emily always seemed to know what to do next. I was intrigued by Karolyn's ability to combine counseling and Christianity. I'd started to entertain the idea of becoming a counselor and giving back what I had been given. The thought seemed to take on new energy after we spoke and I realized that the things I had experienced could be meaningful and helpful to other people.

Some months later, I shared my interest in the counseling field with Karolyn, but quickly added that with a wife and family I didn't see any way I could go back to school for five or six years. She encouraged me to consider chemical dependency counseling. Not only did it specifically address addictive behaviors—something I already knew a lot about—but it required much less schooling. She said it would only take about 2 years to get a chemical dependency professional certificate. I was well aware that it would still be hard to juggle work, family and school, but I couldn't help but get excited. Maybe it WAS something I could do. Maybe this WAS where God was leading me.

Janet . . .

It may be hard to understand why Bruce had such a difficult time letting go of Emily. It is important to remember that not only had she been an understanding ear; a motivator: and someone who accepted him in spite of his past, but she also had opened many new doors and awarenesses to Bruce:

- She helped him slow down the engine of his addiction. Before he started counseling he estimates that 98% of his waking hours (and a good share of his "sleeping ones") were actively spent on his addiction. Now he had days and even weeks where he didn't act out or even feel a desire to act out. He had time to think about and experience a variety of other things.

- She showed him how much he dealt with stress, anger, anxiety and rejection with addictive behaviors and helped him begin to recognize and process the real feelings he had been avoiding all his life.

- She encouraged him to face the reality behind, and of, his actions. She pinpointed what the real problem was and provided him with proof and assurances that he wasn't a perpetrator— that he was turned on by normal things. She encouraged him to find and talk to safe people about his issues, and do responsible things like testing for AIDS, building safeguards into his life and making amends to those he had hurt with his behaviors.

- She helped him acknowledge that he had only been able to see women in two roles: sex objects or mothers (nurturers). If they weren't one he believed they must be the other. She showed him how much he was missing in his relationships by not allowing women the freedom to also be seen as friends, lovers, mentors and co-workers.

- She made him aware of how seriously his family of origin had affected him and that a part of him had been wounded and needed healing. She helped him work through the difficult process of establishing boundaries with his parents and siblings, without putting up walls.

- She taught him to not be so dramatic if he did relapse. All was not lost. He didn't need to beat himself up. He learned it was much more helpful to step back, analyze what had been happening, and see what he could learn from it that would help him in the future.

In some ways, Bruce had gotten from Emily many of the things that he had never been able to get from his mother—acceptance, compassion, consistency. After a lifetime of yearning for these things, it looked as if he was on the verge of losing them yet again. He wrestled with a resurgence of old behaviors as he fumbled, often unsuccessfully, to find healthier ways to deal with the familiar feelings of abandonment. The intensity of his fears knocked him off track, but a loving God drew him back with truth and love. Bruce was only starting to make sense of it all when he wrote this entry in his journal :

Sunday—Feb. 18th
God spoke to me today. I've been angry and depressed for the last 1-1/2 weeks, and I wasn't sure exactly why. I bought some magazines last Friday and then Thursday I spent all day going to x-rated movie theaters.

> *I was angry and tired of dealing with my addiction. I decided not to tell anyone what I was feeling. A wall went up and I became depressed. I wasn't talking to anyone and I was withdrawing. My depression deepened and I was miserable.*
>
> *This morning at church God spoke to me through the sermon. He told me that I needed to make a choice. Either I can have a heavy heart and tell God he's not fair and continue being miserable, or I can choose the truth and pay the heavy price it costs to become the person God wants me to be. It felt like a knife going through my heart when I heard those words and now I feel like a ton of bricks have been taken off of me.*
>
> *It's a long hard road to recovery and sometimes I need to stop and rest and be nourished along the way. God is faithful and has always been there for me. I feel very lucky for this.*

It has been said that God loves us where we are (and the way we are), but he loves us too much to leave us there. God had to close Emily's door so Bruce could see there were other doors opening up to him. God had already made amazing changes in Bruce's life, but there was still much more to do.

18

Finding Answers and Losing Everything

Saying Good-bye to a Marriage

Bruce . . .

During my years of therapy, each of my counselors independently recognized the significant number of symptoms of abuse that I exhibited in my thoughts and actions.

First Gwen and then, in an even greater way, Emily and Karolyn, helped me realize how the unpredictability of my family of origin, and the attitudes and behaviors that they regularly displayed, were a form of abuse and could most certainly cause some of the emotional difficulties that I'd been experiencing. At first it was hard to think of myself as an abuse victim because, even though my growing-up years were usually tumultuous and frequently scary, physical mistreatment —the sort of things that the word "abuse" conjured up in my mind— were virtually non-existent .

In counseling I discovered, however, that a steady diet of the more subtle things that had been going on in our home—the constant fighting between my parents, the erratic moods of my mother, the confusing verbal and non-verbal messages I received— could easily create an unstable environment that would produce the same symptoms in a sensitive child that might be found in someone who had been more violently abused.

NOW CHOOSE LIFE!

This truth helped explain why I had so many classic emotional abuse symptoms: insecurity, depression, emotional numbing, learned helplessness, poor self-esteem, self-loathing, guilt and shame, anger, anxiety, trust difficulties, hypervigilance, fears and phobias, a tendency to isolate, difficulty in saying no to people, emotional dependence on the people I did let into my life and a number of other detrimental manifestations.

What it didn't explain were the other symptoms that I had that were more often associated with physical and sexual abuse: lots of headaches, re-occurring prostate and irritable bowel problems, a generally weakened immune system, sexual issues (both avoidance and addiction), and an inability to be emotionally intimate.

Karolyn, with her background in helping abuse survivors, concentrated on finding the source of these specific symptoms. As with most people with difficult backgrounds, many of my memories were, at first, incomplete. It was like I had still photos for memories instead of movies. For example, when Karolyn asked me to describe one of my earliest childhood memories, I clearly recalled hiding behind the couch with my teddy bear, but I had locked away the painful events that came after it. It wasn't until we began to talk and pray about the initial memory that I began to, little by little, remember more of the story and feel the overwhelming pain and fear that went with the complete memory. It often took numerous sessions and a variety of techniques to remember a whole story and realize its significance.

I always appreciated Karolyn's gentle way of guiding me through this process. She never pushed too hard or suggested any memories or possible conclusions. She allowed me to remember as I was ready. She would simply take me up to the mental and emotional doors I had closed and locked and encourage me to open them. When I got stuck or was too afraid to remember more, we would seek God together for courage and enlightenment.

There were a few times we got a strong sense that the time was not right to pursue a particular path, so we would just let it rest and trust that God would later reveal anything to me that was integral to my recovery. Other times Karolyn would feel God prompting her to utilize hypnosis or other tools to explore some of my sketchier memories.

I remember hypnosis being weird. Not because it was uncomfortable for me or it didn't work—it often revealed extremely important keys to my recovery—but because the time went so fast when I was "under." My hour session would feel like it had only taken 10 minutes. It always left me feeling a little gypped!

Little by little, as my memories became more complete, things began to make sense. Once I let myself remember and feel the emotions attached to those memories, I could finally ask God to heal the wounds caused by those situations. Sometimes God would instantly take away the intensity of the feelings, other times it would require a process of grieving or getting to a place of being able to forgive those that had hurt me, before I actually felt that freedom.

After nearly two years of intense talking, praying, remembering, crying, grieving and forgiving, we still hadn't run into any memory that would explain the symptoms of physical and sexual abuse that were so evident in my life. Karolyn suggested that it was possible that they might just be a product of the attitudes about sex that were verbalized in my home. That explanation never really satisfied me though. It felt like there was something more, but I had no idea what it could be.

At one point Karolyn suggested that I might get something out of a sexual abuse survivor's group that she was facilitating. Since I would be the only man in the group, she asked each of the other current participants whether they thought they would be able to handle me being there. Even though they all said yes, it was extremely uncomfortable for me at first.

I was so afraid that they wouldn't accept me or that my presence would somehow trigger some negative reaction in them. After just a few meetings, however, they realized I wasn't a monster, forgot I was a man and received me into their group. As time went by, I was continually surprised at how similar the issues, feelings and intimacy problems they were experiencing were to the struggles I was having.

Each week Karolyn would present a short teaching about some aspect of sexual abuse recovery and everyone would share their reaction to what she had said or where they were at in relation to the topic. I identified with everything they were saying and shared many of the same symptoms that they talked about, which made not having a specific memory even more frustrating. I couldn't keep from wondering where all my deep and intense feelings were coming from. Part of me was afraid to know the answer, but I also envied those that did have memories because they had something definite to work on. All I could say was "Hi, I'm sexually screwed up and I don't even know why."

Then, after spending several years of intense work with Karolyn relating to my family issues, attending a few different sexual abuse survivor groups, and reading just about everything I could get my hands on about abuse of all kinds[8], I began to experience a substantial amount of generalized anxiety. By now I was familiar with the unshakable feelings of impending doom that would often be present prior to God revealing or expanding an incomplete memory.

The anxiety continued to get worse as the days went by. At my next session with Karolyn we prayed about my intense feelings. During the prayer Karolyn indicated that God was telling her that He was ready to reveal something to me if I was willing. I remember the strange sense of feeling apprehensive and relieved all at the same time. I was scared of what He might tell me, but eager to get rid of the anxiousness.

As I nodded that I was ready, and started asking God to tell me what I needed to know, I began to see a "picture"— like a little movie—in my mind. First I saw a baby that I knew instantly was me. My mother was there and was in the process of changing my wet pants. As she pulled off my soiled diaper, she noticed that I had an erection. I understand now that this is not uncommon for babies and can happen even in utero, but my mom went ballistic. She started ranting and raving and frantically trying to stuff my penis back into my body. I could actually feel the pain of her actions. God assured me that she was not just being mean. She was afraid. He told me that she had been sexually abused herself and seeing my erection had brought back all the ghosts she had never dealt with in her own life.

Even though I was crying and shaking from what had just been revealed to me, it made sense. It finally felt right. No wonder I had had such a hard time remembering. I had been too young. Too young to remember, but definitely not too young to be affected by what had happened. Without God revealing this to me, there would have been no way to get past it.

My mom passed away before I could figure out how to bring up the topic with her, so I never was able to have what I saw confirmed, but I know that that vision, or whatever you want to call it, was a huge turning point in my recovery. Things changed for me after that and my healing began to pick up speed.

Unfortunately, even though I was making great strides in my personal life, things weren't going so well at home. In a lot of ways recovery had been harder on my marriage than my addiction had been. Kathy had been incredibly supportive in the beginning, but no one was able to prepare her for the length of the process.

By now I had been in recovery for almost nine years and it had been a rocky road. When I was first trying to stop acting out sexually, I had failed a lot and between the failures I had leaned heavily on other activities like spending and eating to soothe myself. For a time it was almost as if I had traded addictions.

Then, as I began to dig deeper into the roots of my behaviors, I experienced a significant amount of anger and depression which couldn't have been fun to live with. Sometimes, it was all I could do to just keep my own head above water as I slogged through the sadness and confusion. I know I couldn't have been there for my family in the way that they needed at those times and the fact that I was working swing shift kept me even more isolated from the daily lives of my wife and kids.

There was a point where I realized that Kathy didn't respect me anymore. I knew we had lost something and I didn't know how to get it back. We weren't doing much together anymore. For all intents and purposes, while I was busy with recovery, Kathy had started looking outside our marriage for things to keep her busy and fulfilled. She took up line-dancing and making beer—neither of which I was interested in. She spent more and more time hanging out with her friends and talking on the phone. She was still working full-time at the bakery, and yet she was spending an ever-increasing number of evenings and weekends at home making cakes for her side business. There was less and less time left for me. It made me even more sad and lonely. I fell back into my old spending habits to try to make myself feel better, but all my "retail therapy" only added more stress to an already stressed marriage.

Things finally came to a head late that summer. We had plans to go away for a long-overdue weekend, but while she was packing, Kathy stumbled upon an old stash of pornography that I had long since hidden away. The minute she saw the magazines she said "That's it! I'm done! You need to move out!" There was no discussion—just an ultimatum and I guess I was just too tired of it all to fight it.

It took me a week or so to find a furnished studio apartment in town. The new place was very small, so I couldn't take much, but I bought some used pots and pans and dishes at a garage sale and packed up a few of my personal things. The day I finally left. Kathy was in the kitchen crying. I remember standing in the doorway for a few minutes. "So you're not going to give me any more chances?", I asked. Without even looking up she said, "No." I said "OK", and closed the door on life as I had known it for 23 years.

Sitting alone in my apartment later that night, all the old feelings of rejection flooded in on me. I felt incredibly lonely and isolated and then I remembered God speaking to me alone in my living room nearly ten years before. "Bruce, is your house more important to you than I am? Is your wife more important than I am? How about your children? Are your children more important than I am? There is a very *difficult time coming up when all those things will be in jeopardy and all you have is me."*

I realized that day had come. All I had left was Him.

Janet . . .

Having the symptoms of abuse does not always indicate a history of actual abusive events. Sometimes the same symptoms can be brought on by a perceived event, a misunderstanding of what has happened, or even a prevailing attitude. The details of what did or did not happen are not nearly as important as it is to acknowledge that an individual has been affected by something and needs to deal with those effects.

For the vast majority of sex addicts, however, real abuse seems to be an extremely common occurrence. Patrick Carnes estimates that 74% of sex addicts have been physically abused; 81% have been sexually abused and almost all (97%) have been emotionally abused. Interestingly enough, his studies also show that the same is true of their wives.

Probably at least partially due to this high incidence of abuse and its relating trauma, we find it quite normal for the men we work with that struggle with sexual addiction to have somewhat limited memories of childhood. When they are asked to document the major events in their lives, many of them initially comment that they don't have very many memories that they think would be of value. Like Bruce, almost without exception, once they begin talking about the memories that they do have, additional details and events begin to come to their minds.

Even those that believe they have absolutely no memories of their early childhood usually remember a significant event when God is invited to remind them of anything that would be helpful in their healing process. Many times the events that are remembered are not earth-shaking, but they are almost always important. The mundane events in our lives tend to fade from our memory, but events that were particularly traumatic, exciting or special are usually retained somewhere in our brain awaiting retrieval. If the memories have the potential to cause extreme fear or emotional pain, we may subconsciously avoid acknowledging them and therefore escape feeling the full extent of the emotions attached to them. It requires an extremely supportive environment for someone to feel safe enough to look at memories that they have locked away. Bruce's long-term relationships with his counselors provided the kind of environment that made it safe for him to risk revisiting his most intimidating memories.

It was interesting that the more healing he was able to get emotionally, the less frequently he experienced the illnesses and physical problems that had plagued him throughout his life. These unexpected changes helped confirm to him that he was on the right track.

As mentioned before, the healing of the underlying causes for addictive behaviors is a long and difficult procedure. New research and tools may help expedite the process, but healing still comes one memory at a time. Without an understanding of this, many addicts and their spouses give up before they are able to enjoy the fruit of their hard work.

When months turn into years of intense recovery work, it is hard not to wonder if life will ever be "normal" again. Many spouses start feeling resentful that it has been "all about the recovering addict" and their needs for so long. They question whether they will ever get "their turn" again. If both the spouse and the addict do not have realistic expectations and a strong and helpful support network that cares for the couple as well as the individuals, it is not unusual for the marriage to become a casualty, as it did in Bruce's case.

19

Sex Talk at Church?

More Healing Through God's People

Bruce...
I missed my house. I missed my family. I missed the idea of "belonging" somewhere. In spite of all the counseling I had received and all the hard recovery work I'd done, the separation turned my world upside down and brought me face to face with my old feelings and fears about being unlovable.

Not only had the only woman I'd ever risked letting into my heart decided that I was no longer acceptable, but our break-up seemed to set off a chain of events that sent me plummeting toward depression.

Everywhere I turned, I was an outsider. My church had been Kathy's family church. My friends had been Kathy's friends. My family was virtually gone—my parents had died, my siblings were talking to Kathy more than they were me, my in-laws had closed ranks around their daughter and even my children didn't have time for me. Without a TV, video game system or money to do anything, my kids had declared that my apartment was "too boring" and after only one visit, my son refused to even come stay with me any more. My daughter came occasionally but, as much as I enjoyed her visits, they only intensified the grief I felt at the loss of daily contact and knowing what was going on in their lives.

Instead of our comfortable three-bedroom rambler full of memories and belongings, I now came home to a dinky studio apartment that I could hardly afford to keep. Money was so tight with two households to support, that it was looking more and more like Kathy and I would be forced to file bankruptcy to get out from under the load of debt we were accumulating. It was only a matter of time before my good credit rating would be added to my growing list of losses.

I found myself returning to some of my old habits to keep from having to experience the waves of ugly emotions that kept washing over me. After nearly ten years of recovery it appeared that I had taken many, many steps backward since Kathy had asked me to leave. The only thing that kept me from going totally out of control with the old addictive behaviors was my serious lack of money.

I did my best to fight the urge to act out but, particularly when I was feeling depressed, pornography became an all-too-regular companion once again. I didn't give up on recovery or on God, but my struggle certainly intensified.

The lonely weeks turned into lonely months and before I knew it, I'd been out of the house for an entire year. It had been such a confusing and depressing time. Sometimes it seemed like there might be a glimmer of hope for reconciliation when Kathy would be friendly and flirty. But then, the very next time I saw her, she would be cold and distant and the end seemed inevitable. It made it hard to know what was happening—hard to move on. She'd filed for divorce, but things weren't progressing very quickly and I certainly wasn't trying to push it through. I wanted my family back, but I felt like that decision and the power to make it happen had been snatched out of my hands. There seemed to be nothing I could do but wait and see what choices other people made for MY life.

Even though it was an incredibly bleak time, God still managed to slide a few good things my way. During the time I'd been seeing her for counseling, Karolyn had taken a job on the staff of a local church as their Congregational Care Director. One day, knowing I'd basically been without a church home since the separation, she suggested I come visit her church some Sunday morning and see what I thought. Almost instantly it felt like home. Slowly, as I returned week after week, I began to "plug in", meet people and build a new "family" for myself at the church. Being affiliated with the church also made it possible for Karolyn to give me a reduced fee that allowed me to continue my counseling with her. What a blessing! I would never have been able to keep up my therapy sessions during this difficult time without that help.

Even with God's provision, a lack of money continued to be a huge issue. A few years earlier, when a couple of unsuccessful surgeries for extreme carpal tunnel had pretty much brought an end to my janitorial career, I had followed my dream and gone back to school to become an addiction counselor. By now I'd gotten through my schooling and internship and had my license but, as a beginning counselor, I still didn't make enough money to be starting life over from scratch in my mid-40s. I had taken almost nothing with me when I left the house because I didn't want the kids to do without any of the things they were used to and the few collectible guns and personal things Kathy had let me store in her garage had since been vandalized and stolen. It seemed like every last trace of my old life was being obliterated.

The more I lost, the more meaningful the restoration promises in Joel 2:25 became to me: "I will repay you for the years the locusts have eaten— the great locust and the young locust, the other locusts and the locust swarm—my great army that I sent among you. You will have plenty to eat, until you are full, and you will praise the name of the Lord your God, who has worked wonders for you. . ."

Before He got to restoring the tangible things, however, God still had more restoration to do in my heart.

About a year after Kathy and I split up, Karolyn started talking about a training she and a friend were planning to attend up in Canada. Desert Stream Ministries, a group originally from California had developed a program they called Living Waters that focused on sexual and relational healing. She said she had heard amazing testimonies from the group and was excited about the possibility of offering this sort of deep healing program at our church.

When she got back from the training she was absolutely pumped. She said that in all her years as a Christian she had never experienced anything like it. I found myself catching her excitement as she described a Bible-based program steeped in prayer and truth and grace. She talked about the concept of wounded healers—leaders who walked beside you seeking God for their own healing as they helped you seek Him for yours.

That fall twenty of us, with all kinds of different issues, gathered together in one of the lady's homes to begin another phase of our healing. The program was hard. The teaching and ministry times brought up a lot of emotions. It was the kind of thing that you hated, but couldn't get enough of. Touching those deep wounded places certainly didn't make you feel good, but it felt real and unlocked such important awarenesses. I started to learn how to open the locked doors of my heart and let the Holy Spirit minister to the scared and broken parts of me.

Each week after the teaching we would break up into small groups to discuss the material and how God was making it real to us. As I sat with this same group of men week after week, watching them learn to open up to each other, I realized that this was the substance of a promise God had given to me years earlier while I was still deep in my addiction—before I was really even ready to go for help. I had cried out in my pain and asked God to help me stop my behaviors and he had told me so clearly that I needed to talk to someone. He went on to say that I would ultimately find healing in the church. At the time I couldn't even imagine ever being able to admit my struggle to another living person let alone anyone in the church. I was convinced that I if I did, I would find judgment and rejection instead of the grace and healing God spoke of. But here I was, years later, confessing my struggle and finding love, encouragement and understanding in the midst of God's people.

Although it was scary, it felt good to be surrounded by people who knew my struggle and supported me in my quest for healing. Even though God had brought me wonderful, accepting counselors, I had always felt so alone and alienated in my recovery. I felt uniquely damaged—uniquely sinful. I didn't realize that people all around me had their own broken areas that needed mending, as well.

Even though this was my first experience in opening up to people who weren't counselors or in recovery for their own sexual addiction, I found a strange comfort in the fact that I was surrounded by people that were courageously admitting and facing their own struggles. Even though we were in a Christ-centered environment, we could get past what was "proper" and talk truthfully and pray with one another about our fears, our anger, and even our sexual brokenness. For the first time in forever, I felt less alone—less of a freak.

Janet . . .

In our isolated "I can do it myself" society, we often lose sight of the importance that God places on community. He intended for us to be social beings living in harmony and showing one another sympathy and compassion[9]. In fact, Jesus, himself, told us that loving our neighbors is one of the greatest commandments, second only to loving God himself[10].

Paul further instructs us to rejoice with those who rejoice and mourn with those that mourn[11]. To be able to do that we must become intimate with each other—not sexually—but in that "knowing and being known" sense we talked about briefly in Chapter 7.

It is difficult and scary for any of us to reveal our true self—especially our weaknesses—to another person. We risk being misunderstood, judged, or even rejected. Our disclosures could be ridiculed or used against us. It is a frightening proposition that is even more terrifying for a sex addict. In fact, sexual addiction is frequently called an intimacy disorder because it makes it nearly impossible for someone to take those risks. Most often the addiction had its beginnings as a response to the experience or perception that other people can't be trusted to meet their needs.

All addiction, by its very nature, is isolating. The focus increasingly becomes getting back to the "safety" of whatever behavior or chemical we have chosen to numb ourselves with, and less and less on building mutually beneficial relationships with others. The deeper we get involved in addictive behaviors the more we fear that someone will discover our secret life, and the more we close ourselves off from those around us and hide. In doing so we cheat ourselves out of the encouragement, support and love God has provided for us through His people. Instead of finding and taking our place in the body of Christ[12] where we will experience acceptance and fulfillment, we try, unsuccessfully, to take care of all of our own needs. We lose our sense of belonging and the benefit of the wisdom and clarity that can come from verbalizing our fears and frustrations.

Some of you may remember the movie "Castaway." In the film, Tom Hanks plays a plane crash survivor stranded alone on a tropical island. As resourceful as he was, he struggled to deal with meeting his basic daily needs for food, water, shelter, and medical care. He becomes increasingly frustrated by the challenges life is throwing him. Eventually, quite by accident, he creates a companion out of scavenged items.

Just being able to talk and relate to something actually helps his thinking become clearer and more focused. Even though it is an inanimate object, and his conversations were one-sided, just being able to bounce things off his imaginary buddy helped him find better and quicker solutions. The sense of not being alone gave him the resolve to keep on trying.

We need others to encourage us in life and to gently draw us back when we get off track[13]. This is what Bruce found in Living Waters. It was a place that he could experience something different than he had experienced growing up. It was safe to share his darkest secrets without worrying about condemnation or rejection.

Unfortunately, the attitudes we find in many of our churches encourage people to stay isolated and hidden. The Christian community has a long history of "shooting their wounded." Nowhere is that more evident than in the area of sexual sin. Denial of the problem; hellfire speeches, name-calling, blaming, and lectures only add to the shame and self-loathing already experienced by nearly all sex addicts.

Instead of ministering God's love and freedom, these tactics add yet another lock on the struggler's prison. It, in truth, aids the enemy's plan to destroy our men (and increasingly our women) through sexual sin. Unless the "church universal" wakes up and gains an understanding of the truth about sexual struggles, they can never hope to help the growing number of sexual strugglers in their midst find true victory in Christ.

All too often, there is a belief that once you have given your life to Christ, all your struggles should go away. The basis of this comes from a misunderstanding of the distinct difference between salvation and sanctification.

Salvation is a free gift that God gives to each of us. By simply acknowledging Him as our savior, instead of relying on ourselves, he offers us eternal life and the promise of heaven. Sanctification, however, is the lifelong process of becoming more like Christ. It is hard work that comes only through learning to trust God and others with our deepest fears and most shameful secrets.

20

Burned to Serve

Losing the Shame that Paralyzes

Bruce...
As important as Living Waters was to my recovery, I still felt like something was missing. The weekly teaching had moved and enlightened me. The symbolism of the ministry times had touched my emotions. I had uncovered and examined a lot of painful areas in my life, and I had tasted the freedom that only comes from being able to share your deepest secrets with others— but it still didn't seem to be enough. Even though I had gained a lot of understanding through the lengthy series, deep down I knew that my heart hadn't changed. I still felt like the same wretched excuse for a person I'd always been.

In the spring, ten of us from the group attended a conference that Desert Stream was holding in southern California. The sessions were amazing. Andy Comiskey, the founder of Desert Stream Ministries and creator of the Living Waters program was a dynamic speaker, and we hung on his every word. The worship was incredible—the presence of the Holy Spirit was so strong. Being a part of over 500 people lifting their hands and their voices in song was like experiencing a taste of heaven.

But, things were decidedly different once we went back to our hotel in the evening. I was the only man that had come from our group, so I had a room all to myself. Some people might think that it was a good deal, but it sure didn't work for me. Such exciting things were happening during the day and then I'd go back to my room and have nobody to share them with. I tried to read. I tried to pray. But, I just couldn't settle down. I felt so lonely and isolated.

At breakfast I would hear the women talking about the deep discussions they'd had after hours and I felt even more alienated. Once again, I was the outsider. It's hard to put into words the desolation of always feeling like you're on the outside looking in—but that's what was happening yet again. It finally got so unbearable that I went to Karolyn and told her how depressed and upset I was. I confessed that I was having a miserable time and just wanted to go home. We talked a bit and then she suggested that I give what I was feeling to God.

> *"Father, I'm feeling horrible here and I don't know what to do. Everything in me wants to run away. My whole life I've felt alone and alienated just like I'm feeling now. It's too familiar. It hurts too much. It feels so hopeless. I want to give all these awful thoughts and emotions to you. Do whatever you want with them. I've tried so hard, but I just can't fight them anymore. I need your help . . . "*

After spilling my guts out to God, I went back to my room, but I couldn't see where the prayer had made a bit of difference in my life. I didn't feel any relief—no peace—no buoyed spirits. I just felt depressed. In fact, I had never been to a conference that I hated quite so much. My only solace was that there were only a few more days to endure, and then I could go home and be done with it.

I didn't sleep very well that night and barely drug myself through breakfast the next morning. Everybody took so long to get ready to leave the hotel that our group arrived at the church late, just as everyone was gathering for the worship time. We were barely able to slip into some empty seats before the band began to play the intro for the first song[14]. I wasn't familiar with what they were singing, but I was sure I recognized some of the words as scripture[15].

"... I see the Lord, He is high and lifted up.

Angels cry holy, holy is the Lord..."

There was something haunting about the melody. We rose to our feet and, as I began to worship God, I felt His overwhelming presence come down on me. I could barely stay standing. My legs buckled under my body and I had to grab on to the chair in front of me to keep from crashing to the floor. I crumpled to my knees and then down to the ground. I couldn't move—all I could do was lay there and take in the song. It was as if God was searing each word into my heart.

"... I see the Lord and His eyes are flaming like fire..."

I was afraid to be in the presence of such incredible holiness. I felt like I needed to hide. I was so sinful—how could God even look on me? But, at the very same time, I felt embraced by a love so powerful that it pushed away my fear. My sin began to feel smaller and smaller. It was as if I had been straining to climb a huge mountain that suddenly turned into a molehill right under my feet. In the presence of God's love my sin seemed miniscule. I was totally blown away.

"... The angel came and touched the coal to my lips.
My guilt is gone and my sin has been forgiven..."

As I listened to the words of the song, I felt like I was experiencing them with God at the very same time. I felt a heat go through my body like a flame. I was sure it was doing something, but I didn't know what. I just knew I was changing somehow. I was crying and trying to sing along but nothing would come out— I couldn't even talk. All I could do was mouth the words.

> *". . . And the temple is filled with the glory of God*
> *And the whole earth is filled with the glory of God . . ."*

I was no longer depressed. I was in absolute awe. Overwhelmed. I felt like I could take on anything with the power I was feeling from God. It was so different than what I had been feeling when I came in the building just a few minutes earlier.

> *". . . He called to me "Whom shall I send?"*
>
> *I answered Him "I will go for You . . ."*

I squeaked out an echo "I will go for You." And I meant it. I knew without a doubt that God had just called me out in an unforgettable way to minister to people struggling with the same thing that I was struggling with. I was ready and willing to do anything God asked me to do.

But I also knew in my heart that something else, even bigger, had just happened inside of me. I just couldn't put my finger on what it was . . . yet.

Janet . . .

Before he even left California, Bruce bought a Vineyard CD containing the song that God had used to speak so powerfully to him. Every time he listened to it he would find himself tearing up and feeling some of the same emotions that he felt that first time. Once home, he discovered that the words of the song had come almost verbatim from a passage in Isaiah. It was almost three months later, however, before he understood what else God had done during what he was now calling his "Isaiah 6 experience."

It became evident to him when he had another small "slip" with pornography. By now he was following God's call and acting as a co-leader for one of the small groups at Living Waters. A part of the accountability and healing process that had been set out for leaders necessitated that they confess their struggles and slips to the group they were leading. Bruce said it was hard to get up and tell them that he had failed, but in doing so, he realized that he no longer felt the debilitating shame that he had felt when he had acted out before. He was still remorseful. He was still sad. He was still a bit embarrassed. But he didn't feel disgusting. It was obvious that God had burned away the heavy load of shame that he had always carried around with him.

There are two types of shame that we can encounter in our lives. With the first kind, we feel shame (or ashamed) because we have done something wrong. It is healthy and most often leads to repentance and a stronger relationship with God and others.

But, there is another sort of shame that is much more sinister—toxic shame. This shame doesn't just tell us that our actions or choices are bad. It tells us WE are bad.

A person that is experiencing toxic shame believes that there is some inherent flaw in them that makes them worse—more sinful—more detestable— than anyone else. It causes them to want to hide and isolate from other people. Instead of leading to repentance and healing, it creates hopelessness. People with toxic shame sincerely believe that something in their core is bad and that, no matter what they do or how hard they try, that badness is still going to be there. It keeps them from even trying to change.

A year or so before this experience, Bruce had expressed frustration in his journal at not being able to be completely "real" in a lot of situations.

> *Tuesday—February 13th*
> *Honesty is absolutely necessary for recovery, however, not so easy to practice. I have not been honest or held accountable for my actions lately. I hide the real me in the groups I attend. Fear and lack of trust are holding me back. I have heard others in AA & NA that are sharing at a level of honesty that I have not been able to attain.*

NOW CHOOSE LIFE!

He said he could share history —the struggles and failures that had happened in the past—but not what was happening in the here and now. After the toxic shame was burned away, two significant things happened:

1. Bruce was more able to talk about a struggle while he was still in it. Verbalizing the cravings and old thinking he was experiencing often took their power away. When the cravings were less intense, he was able to make different, better choices about how to deal with them, usually without acting out at all. And, if a slip did happen, it could be seen and used as a learning tool, instead of a reason to hate himself even more.

2. Removing the shame also gave Bruce the freedom to reach out to others. It would have been nearly impossible to stand up publicly and share his story with others if he still felt that he was uniquely and irreversibly flawed. He couldn't have been as honest or as effective as a leader without this experience that finally let him separate his actions from his value.

Without fail, when God calls us to do something, he also empowers us to do the job.

Part Three:

Finally Discovering the Path to Life

You make known to me the path of life;
you will fill me with joy in
your presence,
with eternal pleasures at
your right hand.
Psalm 16:11

21

What God Promises, He Does

God Restores What the Locusts Have Eaten

Bruce . . .

In one of my prayer times soon after the separation, God promised me that He would restore what the locusts had eaten just like He talked about in the 2nd Chapter of Joel. Several years had slipped by and, as much as I had hung onto that promise, I sure hadn't seen any signs of anything being restored to me.

The divorce had happened. The bankruptcy had happened. And because of them, I had been pretty much forced to abandon the studio apartment and start renting a room in a co-worker's basement. I hated living there. It was dark, depressing, and noisy, but at least it was finally something I could afford.

I had my job and I still went to Living Waters and was involved in a Bible study, but the rest of the week, and especially on the weekends, I had a hard time getting used to not being part of a family. I could seldom afford to go anywhere, and even when I could, I really didn't enjoy doing things alone, so most of the time I just sat at home and looked at the four dreary walls of my "dungeon."

I was feeling particularly down about the state of my life at one of my counseling sessions with Karolyn. I was depressed and lonely and was bellyaching about how I'd probably never meet anybody,

I'd probably never have money again, and I'd have to live like a mole—underground and alone in the basement— forever. Once I was through with my venting, we prayed, as we always did at the end of a session. After the prayer, Karolyn excitedly shared that God had told her that he was preparing a woman for me. I remember laughing at her and saying "yeah, right, Karolyn." If it was a message from God—and I had my doubts—He sure wasn't in any hurry to show His work.

In the next six months things got even worse. I was laid off from my job when a frivolous lawsuit against the facility I was working for prompted them to close down my entire unit AND, right on the tails of that, the family I was renting the room from decided to put their house on the market. Without warning, I suddenly had no job and housing that could end at any time. It seemed like those locusts just couldn't get enough of my life. They kept eating and eating until they had consumed nearly everything in sight.

Now that I was only a few steps away from being homeless and penniless, I decided to take a free job search skills class that was being offered by a local agency that helped people find employment. The class was every day for three weeks. I'm not sure how helpful it was in honing my skills, but at least it got me out of the house and gave me something different to think about. As the class progressed, I found myself becoming fascinated by one of the women that was attending. She was outgoing and friendly. The best way to describe Janice was as the "cruise director" type. She was always recruiting people for her latest adventure—whether it was getting a bunch of us together to grab a cheap lunch or working on some job search project together. She had the gift of motivating people. She also had a lot of energy and was a ton of fun. One day she and I teamed up to practice our interviewing skills for class. After we did the exercises, our talk turned to more personal things. We found out that we had a lot in common. We were both Christians, both divorced, both had two kids, both without a job, and both trying to get our feet back under us. She talked about a class she was taking that looked at dating and marriage from a Christian perspective and I told her about Living Waters and a divorce recovery group that Karolyn was going to be starting in a few weeks. She seemed really interested and asked whether it was open to people outside my church. She thought that some of the people from her dating class might be interested in attending.

A few weeks later, on the first night of the divorce group—there she was, with a friend in tow. I was excited about the chance to get to know her a little better. I hadn't really done any dating since my divorce, but Janice got me thinking that it might be nice. Maybe it was time to do something about the loneliness I'd been feeling. The divorce recovery group had rules against participants dating during the fourteen-week class, so it wasn't really an option yet . . . but there was definitely a growing interest on my part.

As the weeks went by I watched and listened intently to the things Janice said in the group. She had some interesting ideas and opinions. But, quite unexpectedly, I also found myself being intrigued by some things I heard her friend say. She seemed to have such a hunger to get beyond the painful things in her life and not stay stuck. She echoed the desires of my own life.

A month or two into the class Janice kicked into her regular cruise-director mode and tried to get a bunch of us together to go to the County Fair. She suggested that anybody who wanted to go could meet at the mall parking lot Saturday morning and we would all carpool the rest of the way. Of course, I was rarin' to go—it sure beat spending another Saturday alone and it would give me the opportunity to see Janice in a more casual social setting.

Nobody was in the mall parking lot yet when I arrived on Saturday, but it wasn't long before Janice's friend from our group drove up in a shiny red Toyota. I remembered that her name was Janet. Our whole divorce class had been having trouble keeping Janice and Janet's names straight, even though the two of them were nothing alike. Janet was much quieter and more introverted than Janice. She was also quite a bit taller and had a highly infectious laugh and a welcoming smile. I climbed out of the truck to say hello and we chatted awkwardly until Janice finally showed up, followed closely by another woman and her daughter. The five of us waited a bit and when no one else came, we all loaded into the woman's van and headed out to the fair.

We had a great day wandering around looking at the exhibits and the animals, eating greasy junk food, and enjoying the live music. Everything about it just felt good. Janet and I ended up spending a lot of the day together, as the others scurried to see people or things that were of interest only to them. I enjoyed our time together, but I felt a bit sorry for her, too. She seemed so hesitant to spend any money—even for lunch. I couldn't figure it out. Her car couldn't have been more than a couple years old, she dressed nicely, but yet she acted as if she was extremely poor. I figured she must not have a very good job or else she'd be loading up on food and trinkets like the rest of us. She was a lot of fun, however and, once we got past the initial self-consciousness, I found she was really easy to talk to, as well.

After that first outing, Janice, Janet and I did something almost every weekend—sometimes with other people, sometimes just the three of us. We went to movies, plays, dinners, and other local events. Other times, we would go to Janet's house to watch a video or just talk over a cup of herbal tea. It was so nice to have interesting things to look forward to and enjoyable people to do them with.

As great as all this new-found activity was, a new problem soon arose that both surprised and confused me. I found myself becoming increasingly attracted not only to Janice, but to Janet as well. It was the first time I'd had an interest in the opposite sex since the separation and divorce and it was scary and exciting all at the same time. I certainly didn't know what I was doing or how to proceed with either one of them. I hadn't dated in years—and I hadn't even done all that much of it back then. My fixation with pornography throughout high school and college had kept me from taking risks with real relationships, so now, as a grown adult, I didn't know what to do with my interest. I didn't have a clue how to get the ball rolling. I had never learned how.

In the process of struggling to sort things out, I talked to Karolyn about my feelings for "the Jans." She encouraged me to talk to them and tell them how I felt. The whole idea terrified me. I wasn't sure what their reaction would be. I certainly didn't want to risk ruining the great thing we had going.

With Karolyn's persistent prodding, I finally mustered the courage to tell them I "liked" them both, one day over sub sandwiches. It was so difficult to put my feelings out on the table like that, but I spoke my piece and held my breath while I waited to see what would happen. Unfortunately, neither one of them seemed to comprehend that I was saying I was interested in them in a romantic way. They just kind of looked at me, like they would have looked at their brother, and nonchalantly said "yeah, we like you too, Bruce" and went on with the conversation. I was totally deflated. Here I thought I had disclosed this huge earth-shaking declaration and they had totally missed it. I REALLY didn't know what to do with my feelings now. Liking them both was so confusing—what was I supposed to do with that anyway?

As time went by I started to realize that Janet was actually more my style. I liked that she was more of a homebody; more grounded than Janice, who always loved to be going somewhere and doing something. Janice was fun and energetic, but Janet was the kind I could see myself settling down with.

Not long after I had that realization, Janice got a job at an airline reservation center. She started working odd shifts and was seldom available to do things with us any more. In my mind it was God's perfect timing. Janet and I didn't need a cruise director to get us up and out of the house any longer—doing things together had become such a habit that neither one of us even considered stopping. And, as much fun as Janice had always been, I was thrilled to be able to spend more time alone with Janet.

I found it a bit bizarre that even though we had already spent hours and hours together, the first time we ventured out by ourselves felt a little strange and awkward. In some ways it seemed more like a date when it was just the two of us—and a big part of me wished it was—but we still had one more hefty roadblock to get past before that could happen.

Months earlier Janet had started coming to church and our singles events with me. Her house was only a few miles down the road from the apartment I had just moved into, so it was easy for me to swing by and pick her up. Although we would chat happily on the ride to wherever we were going, once we arrived she was always very cognizant of not appearing like a couple. She would sit a few feet away from me in the pew or spend the evening chatting with people across the room at social events. At one point I heard her tell her grown son that I was "like the brother she'd never had." Part of me was crushed—I wanted to be more than a brother to her, but the other part of me understood where she was coming from. Almost since I had known her, Janet had been talking about the feelings she had for one of the other guys at church. She had met him at the same divorce recovery group where we had met and although they had never dated, he was part of the "gang" we often hung around with. She definitely had a crush on him and he was certainly friendly with her—it just never seemed to go anywhere.

I would often lend an ear to her as she wrestled to understand the mixed messages she was getting from him. One day he would be friendly and attentive, and the next time she saw him he would hardly give her the time of day. She was having a hard time figuring out where she stood and whether she had a chance with him or not. The more I grew to care about her, the more difficult it was to stand by and watch her settling for the pitiful crumbs he threw her way. I wanted more for her.

When I shared my dilemma with Karolyn, she counseled me to be patient and see what happened. She and I talked and prayed about it often after that. It was such a difficult situation. Janet and I got along so well together. We had great talks and great fun and, deep down, I desperately wanted a chance to show her that there was someone who really DID care for her and would treat her so much better than this guy ever did. But, for some reason, she just couldn't see me as anything but a really good friend. It was painful and frustrating. As intense as my feelings for her had become, I stayed quiet about them, because if she really wanted this guy, I didn't want to be the one to get in the way.

As difficult as it was, I tried to be satisfied laying low and just being friends. In addition to going to church, hanging out watching TV, and going to movies, we started taking a lot of walks as the weather began to improve. Some days we'd walk around the neighborhood, other times we'd go to a park or around the lake. Those walks became special times of sharing that deepened our friendship and trust for each other. We were getting closer and closer, and although I was afraid to get my hopes up, things seemed to be changing between us.

Ever since that first day we spent together at the fair, Janet and I had always hugged goodbye. At the beginning they were just quick, friendly hugs, but as time went by, I was finding it increasingly difficult to let go of her. The hugs were getting longer and longer and for some reason, she wasn't pulling away either. It didn't make sense, but I wasn't complaining. I had never felt this close to anyone. For the first time in my life I was actually experiencing sexual feelings and love for someone at the same time. It was getting harder and harder not to tell her how I felt, but Karolyn kept assuring me that I needed to hold on just a little longer.

One particularly nice spring Saturday Janet and I decided to go on a spontaneous adventure. We stopped by the store, picked up some fried chicken and a few other things and hit the road. We were intent on going no place in particular. We agreed that at each intersection we came to we would take the road that was least familiar to us and see where it took us. We stumbled on a park we didn't know even existed, we drove through miles of rural countryside, we poked around some antique stores and book stores, we laughed and talked and teased each other. It was a perfect day in every way, especially at dinner when Janet announced that she'd been doing a lot of thinking and praying and was convinced that there was no future with the guy she had admired for so long. She said she was done pursuing that relationship and felt a real peace about that decision. My heart actually jumped with joy on hearing her words! Finally I had the green light I had been hoping and praying for.

As luck would have it, it looked like I would have plenty of time to contemplate my next move. Janet was planning to fly out in just a few days to spend ten days with some friends of hers that pastored a church in Arizona. The night before she left, I stopped by her house to wish her a good trip. She took a little break from her packing and we talked for a while.

I knew I was going to miss her terribly, but since we were still "just friends" I couldn't really belabor the point. Instead, I did the next best thing and offered to pick her up at the airport when she got back to town. I was pleased when she accepted my offer, because at least it guaranteed that I'd be seeing her again the minute she returned. I knew she still had packing to do, so as much as I didn't want to leave, I wished her a great trip and gave her an extra long hug. I was surprised and excited when she stroked the hair at the back of my neck during the hug. It felt very special and intimate. Again my heart soared.

While Janet was out of town, I told Karolyn what she had said about giving up on the other guy and how she had run her fingers through my hair while we were hugging. I think she was even more excited than I had been and said that that was definitely a sign that she liked me. It made me wonder whether it was FINALLY time to let her know how I felt.

A week and a half later I was waiting at the airport when Janet's plane arrived. I was so anxious to see her that I felt like a little kid on Christmas morning. I had thought about her so often while she was gone and couldn't wait to give her another hug and hear all about her trip. A few days earlier she had given me a quick call to let me know that nothing had changed with the flight and to reconfirm that I really would be there to pick her up. Hearing her voice made me miss her all the more and it made me sad that she had been let down by so many people in her past that she half expected me to blow her off as well. I was determined to be the one to show her that there were people you could count on in this world. Not everyone promises stuff and then doesn't do it.

I don't know which of us was more excited when her plane finally landed and we caught each other's eye. She looked so relieved that I'd actually shown up and I was just happy that she was finally home. . . and the hug we gave each other felt oh so good!

I could tell that she was tired, so I suggested that I just drop her off at her house and stop by after Bible Study the following night to hear all about her vacation. She agreed, but made me wait while she dug around in her luggage and pulled out a small carved wooden turtle that she had gotten me. Knowing how hard it was for her to spend money made it an even more special that she had brought me a gift. I gave her another hug, and my turtle and I headed for home.

Seeing her again had set my mind in motion. Ever since our adventure day I had been trying to figure out how I was going to talk to her about the way I felt about her. It hadn't seemed right to bring it up while she was busy getting ready to leave for Arizona . . . but now that she was back . . . I knew it needed to be done. I'd talked to Karolyn about it and the people in my Bible Study, but I still didn't know how I was going to do it

The next night at Bible Study we did our normal check in about what was going on in our life and how the last week had been. When it was my turn, all I could talk about was the fact that Janet had gotten back from her trip, how fun it was to pick her up at the airport, how much I had missed her and how cool it was that she had brought me back a gift. All of a sudden the lady who's house we were at interrupted me. "Alright, that's it . . . this meeting is over . . . you get over there and tell her how you feel . . . right now!" I was a little startled, but I knew she was right. It WAS the right time.

I was really scared and nervous as I drove over to Janet's. I didn't know how she would take what I was going to say. I knew, deep down, that once we talked, things would never be the same between us. If it didn't go well it could end our friendship—and I certainly didn't want that. There was no way that I could predict which way it would go, but I was determined to go through with it no matter what.

My hands were shaking and my stomach was churning as I rang the doorbell. Janet looked surprised when she came to the door, "Oh, hi! I didn't expect you so early, did they cancel Bible Study or something?"

"No, not exactly, but I have something I want to talk to you about."

"Oh, okay . . . ya wanna go sit in the family room?" She looked a little apprehensive as we sat down on the couch.

"I don't know how to start this, so I think I'll just get right to the point. I really like you Janet—I have for a very long time— and I want to be more than just friends. I want to date and have a relationship with you and see where it goes. Would that be OK with you?" She seemed a bit stunned. She didn't say anything, she just nodded yes, with the biggest grin on her face. I was so happy and so relieved. I leaned forward and gently kissed her for the first time and then put my arm around her and we leaned back against the couch. We talked for a little while in each other's arms and agreed that we'd move forward slowly and prayerfully and see what happened. It felt good and it felt right.

On my way home I felt absolutely high. I know what they mean when someone says they were "floating on cloud 9" because that's where I was. The minute I got in my door, I called Janet to tell her goodnight. I just wanted to hear her voice one more time and make sure I hadn't been dreaming all of this. The evening had held such a wide range of emotions: fear, anxiety, determination, joy, relief. I was absolutely exhausted, but I was so excited that I still had a hard time getting to sleep. I played our conversation over and over in my mind and every single time it made me smile.

Our vow to "go slow" in building our relationship turned out to be a little hollow. To be honest, we couldn't figure out what going slow would look like. We were already the best of friends. We had a lot of history together and were used to sharing our innermost thoughts, feelings, and goals with each other. We agreed on where we wanted to go in our lives and what we believed was important. Deep down we both instinctively knew that committing to "having a relationship" at this point was a thinly veiled agreement that we would get married. There was only one thing we hadn't talked about, and as near as I could tell, it was the only thing that had the potential to derail the fast- moving train we were on.

Although Janet knew that I was committed to recovery, we had never talked about what I was in recovery from. It just wasn't the kind of thing you talked about with very many people. As we neared the end of our first week as a couple, it was pretty evident that we were quickly heading for the altar. As scary as it was to think about, it was important to me that Janet know EVERYTHING about me before we made that intent official.

I knew in telling her about my past that I was risking everything, again. A full disclosure of my struggle could be a relationship breaker. We had been so happy this past week that I didn't want to rock the boat, but I knew I wouldn't be able to live with myself if I didn't lay it all out on the table. So, we had our second life-changing talk in a week. I told Janet about the turmoil of my growing up years, about my addiction to pornography, and even about the prostitutes. I also shared with her a bit about the recovery process I had been going through for the past twelve years. I did my best to tell her what she was getting into. As I talked, I was surprised to see tears forming in her eyes. I was so afraid that it meant she was going to tell me to leave and never come back but, instead, she put her arms around me and said "I'm so sorry that you had to live through that." The gentle way she said it made me start to cry as well. We held on to each other and cried tears of sorrow about my past, mixed with tears of joy about our future. Then I told her how much healing God had done in my life and how exciting it was to finally have sexual feelings and love for someone at the very same time. I admitted that although I had started to feel glimmers of it with Kathy just before we separated, I had never experienced it so completely with anyone before.

NOW CHOOSE LIFE!

Just a week later I asked Janet—the woman I knew beyond a shadow of a doubt that God had been preparing for me—to marry me. When she said yes, I knew God was finally beginning to restore what the locusts had eaten, just like he had promised.

Janet . . .

Although I have been studying and working with sexual addiction on a professional basis for quite a few years now, I can also speak as a loving wife who has come face to face with the devastating wake of this addiction in my own marriage and home.

I have to admit, that when Bruce first told me about his struggle with sexual addiction, I didn't fully grasp the magnitude of what he was telling me. I came from a world where sexual addiction had been nothing more than a joke. The term "sex addict" was just a label my friends and I would use to describe a guy that was a little too preoccupied with sex—the kind that got a little too "gropey" on a date. I didn't have a clue about the intense pain and isolation that is experienced by those truly struggling with sexual addiction.

Even in today's more "enlightened" society, Bruce and I still regularly encounter people—even some professional counselors—who snicker and joke when sexual addiction is mentioned. We often overhear people remark that "sexual addiction would be the FUN addiction to have."

Neither Bruce, nor any of the men we have worked with, would ever call it a fun addiction. What might have started out as the innocent curiosity of a ten or eleven year old, or later in life as a diversion from the stresses of daily living, quickly became an unrelenting master that ruined both their relationships and their self-esteem. Sexual addiction can be one of the most difficult addictions to overcome, but our God is a miracle-working God.

In fact, without God's amazing choreography, what are the chances that Bruce and I would have ever gotten together? If Bruce and Janice hadn't both lost their jobs at about the same time and heard about the job skills class, they would have never met. If Janice and I hadn't both decided to attend a local seminar for single adults

What God Promises, He Does

and become two of only five of the seminar participants that chose to go on to an optional 6-week processing group, Janice and I would have never met. If Janice and Bruce had never talked, she would have never known about the divorce recovery group at his church. If Janice hadn't told our processing group about the divorce recovery group, I would have never known about it. If I hadn't decided to go to it, Janice wouldn't have been able to introduce me to Bruce...and so on and so on. There were so many opportunities for the chain of events to be broken.

Yes, God was preparing a woman for Bruce . . . but he was also preparing any number of events and encounters to accomplish His plan. The same God that brought all those little pieces together for us can also restore a broken life. Orchestrating what seems impossible is easy for Him.

I'm still amazed that so much had been happening in my life without me even realizing what God was doing. Sure, I was seeking to follow Him, but I certainly didn't have any awareness of all the things that were going on just out of my line of sight. Later, while my eyes were focused on someone else, God created the most incredible and pure friendship between Bruce and I, without romance getting in the way. And when that had been accomplished, God started to open up my heart.

The whole time I was in Arizona I couldn't get Bruce out of my mind. I remember being confused as to why my thoughts kept drifting back to him. After all, we were just friends. I wasn't having the same incessant thoughts about my other friends while I was on vacation. Little did I know that it was just my mind catching up with what had already happened in my heart. I didn't fully realize how intense my feelings were for Bruce until the very minute he asked me about having a relationship. My answer surprised even me. But the minute I agreed, I knew it was right.

As I look back, I can see God's hand in every aspect of our courtship and wedding. Even though we had originally been intent on taking it slow, we ended up getting married just three months after our "talk" at an untraditional potluck gathering of all our dear friends and family. The day became a celebration of not only our relationship, but also of God's restorative work in our individual lives. The counselors that had played such an important part in helping us heal our wounds and begin to prepare for this day, were an integral part of our ceremony.

The panic of having our pastor drop out just days before the wedding because of medical issues, turned into the delightful blessing of being able to be married by my pastor friend and his wife that I had visited in Arizona just a few months earlier. I don't believe it was a coincidence that, unbeknownst to me, they just "happened" to be in our area—at least 1500 miles from their home—on that particular weekend. God loves to bless us with the deepest desires of our hearts—whatever they may be.

22

Turning to an Old Friend

A Little Lapse Creates a Big Obstacle

Bruce...
In the course of just a few months God did, indeed, restore much of what I had lost—a wife, a house, an extended family, good credit (well, Janet's anyway, I was still working on mine), but even the best of times can present unexpected fears and challenges.

Things had fallen into place so quickly, that we had been a little apprehensive about telling our friends and family about our engagement. We were sure that they would caution us about getting married so hastily or maybe even try to talk us out of it. But instead we got responses like, "well, it's about time" or "yeah, we were expecting this." It looked like Janet was the only one that hadn't noticed the sparks between us. The fact that everyone we talked to was so supportive of our marriage was yet another confirmation that it was God's plan for us.

As we catapulted towards our wedding day, I was so excited. Not only was God fulfilling his promise to me, but I was experiencing all sorts of good feelings. Of course there was the giddy happiness of being in love—the same kind I had experienced with Kathy . . . but there was also something more—something that I'd never really felt before. When Janet and I kissed and caressed each other, I felt sexual feelings that melded with the love. Before, those two feelings were completely compartmentalized. I could feel love for someone or I could be sexual with them—but I could never have both together. The only way I could "perform" was to shut off my emotions and just go through the physical actions of sex. My body was there, but my head was lost in some fantasy that kept me a safe distance from real intimacy.

It's a difficult concept for sexually healthy people to understand. They tell me that they don't get how someone can separate sex from love. The two are so tightly integrated for them that they can't fathom one without the other but, for me, sex with someone I loved always brought yucky feelings. It certainly wasn't Kathy's fault. She was attractive and kind and I loved her incredibly—I was just too damaged back then to be able to bring the two things together.

Now, after a dozen years of counseling, I was in new territory. I could feel that deep love for Janet and yet I could still feel aroused at the same time. I was looking forward to all that coming together on our wedding night.

My old addictive behaviors had resurfaced a few times since the divorce, especially when I was feeling particularly lonely, but for the most part, they had remained reasonably under control. It really took me by surprise, when my acting out became more frequent after Janet and I decided to marry. At first I couldn't figure out what it was all about. I was happier than I had been in a long time, but yet the craving to get lost in pornography and masturbation had increased exponentially. I finally realized that even though it felt good to be in a relationship, I had a lot of anxiety about failing again. Ironically, it was the very way I was choosing to handle those fears that had the greatest potential of destroying our relationship before it ever had a chance.

A couple of weeks before the wedding, I was starting to move some of my books, camping gear and other things I wouldn't be needing right away into Janet's house. It was a challenge to integrate my outdoorsy, bachelor things into the Victorian home she had lived in for over 20 years. She was a good sport, however, and made a real effort to find room for my books in her already full bookcase, rework a picture grouping in the family room to receive my prized deer antlers, and squeeze the contents of two closets into one to give me space for my clothing and gun collection. I know the chaos of moving things around drove her nuts, and she had a few mini-meltdowns, but she did a great job of transforming it from her place to OUR home.

At one point during all the hub-bub of moving stuff around, she bent down and picked up a piece of paper that had fallen out of one of my boxes. I saw her face go white as she glanced to see what it was. She didn't say a word as she rushed from the room, but instinctively I knew I should go after her. I found her slumped onto the couch sobbing.

"What is it, kiddo?" I said softly.

She silently thrust out her arm and opened her fist to reveal the crumpled piece of paper. I took it from her and instantly recognized it as a receipt from the adult video store.

"Look at the date." She said, shakily between sobs. "How could you do that? How could you go rent porn on the day before we got engaged?"

"I'm sorry. Really I am. I was just so scared."

"Scared of what? Scared of marrying me?" she snapped painfully through her tears.

"No, of course not, but it's a big commitment. I think it's normal to be a little nervous. I've failed at marriage before and I'm so afraid that I'll do something to screw this up too. I don't ever want to go through that again. I guess I just slipped back into my old way of handling yucky feelings. I really am sorry. I wasn't thinking clearly. I didn't mean to hurt you."

"But I thought you said you were done with this stuff. I thought you said you were healed. Maybe I'm just being stupid again. I don't want to make another mistake either. I thought we had something really special here . . . but I guess I've just been hearing what I wanted to hear. Maybe we should just call this whole thing off before we get in any deeper. "

"C'mon Janet, I said I'm sorry. I made a bad choice. We DO have something special and I HAVE had a lot of healing. Don't give up on me. Don't give up on us. We can work through this. I know we can."

We talked and prayed well into the night and by the time I went home, we were on solid ground once again. It had been a close call, though—too close. I had been so afraid that she would throw in the towel. I didn't want to lose her and felt embarrassed and sad that I had hurt someone else with my addiction—that I had brought this ugliness into yet another relationship.

Janet . . .

I was so torn when I found that pornography receipt that I didn't know which way to turn. I really didn't know whether we should go through with the wedding or not. I couldn't imagine living without Bruce—he seemed to be the guy I'd been waiting for my whole life—but I was desperately afraid of being deceived again. I had been blind and naïve in my past relationships, and I didn't trust that I had any greater ability to see things clearly now.

I'd failed at marriage before. I hadn't wanted a divorce . . . people in my family didn't get divorced . . . in fact, I didn't even BELIEVE in divorce. . . and yet it happened to me not once, but twice. Outwardly, I had done everything "right"—I met both men at church, we did all the things that "good" Christian couples do—we prayed together and ministered together—but, in both cases, I had chosen men that had experienced so much pain and loss in their lives that they didn't know how to do anything but quit when things got rough. It was obvious that my "man-picker" was seriously broken.

Both of my former husbands had seemingly done all the "right" things and said all the "right" things, and yet they left with little concern for me or the kids. It totally destroyed my belief in "face value." After that, I was afraid to trust anything that looked or sounded the least bit suspicious, and even things that appeared good or positive were suspect. What if I was just being blind again? What if it wasn't what it seemed? Allowing myself to have confidence in what I saw or heard seemed like a risk that would only lead to more hurt and disappointment. It made it incredibly difficult to believe the promises Bruce made to me. He had to keep reminding me that he was not those other guys—I could count on him.

But could I? Clutching that dream-shattering receipt, I couldn't discern whether this was really an isolated occurrence like Bruce said it was, or whether I had just fallen for another man's artfully crafted lies. Not being able to trust my own judgment made it extremely difficult to trust another person. Bruce's patience and God's intervention were the only things that gave me the courage to risk moving ahead with the marriage.

Once we got past that incident, we found ourselves again eagerly looking forward to our marriage, but, sadly, that regenerated excitement would also be short-lived. Hardly more than 24 hours after the wedding it would be challenged again.

23

Death Revisited

More Lessons to Learn—This Time Together

Bruce . . .
Just weeks after God rescued our relationship, our wedding was as unique as our courtship had been. We had chosen a relaxed setting for our ceremony so we would have the opportunity to share our personal testimony of God's hand on our lives. Many of our guests had walked beside us through some of our most difficult days, so it seemed only right for them to be a part of this victorious celebration—to hear and see the outcome of all their prayers and support.

Janet and I shared the special promise verses God had given to each of us during our bleakest times. Mine, of course, was the one about restoring what the locusts have eaten; hers was Jeremiah 29:11-13 where God declares that he has plans to prosper us and give us hope and a future. We spoke of God's faithfulness and healing power that brought us to a place where we could finally receive the fruit of those promises.

The song—our song— that Janet's son and daughter sang at our wedding spoke eloquently about the relationship God had given us. Even though neither one of us are real country music fans, Lonestar's song, "Amazed"[16] expressed our feelings so well. I remember getting goosebumps the first time Janet played it for me.

Predictably, the song spoke of the intensity of our love, but it also focused on something else that, as a recovering sex addict, was totally new to me. It talked about feeling so close to someone that you were able to see inside of them and share their thoughts and dreams.

Having spent most of my life in shame, hiding and numbness, the whole idea of allowing myself to feel and share at that level was foreign to me. Discovering that I was actually starting to be able to experience it—like the song said—was absolutely amazing!

There is another part of the song that tells of being blown away by the love that was emanating from the other person. I realized that, for the first time, I was healed enough that I, too, could let a little bit of that love seep in.

Both Janet and I WERE absolutely blown away by what God had done in bringing us together. In spite of our fears and even our missteps, everything was so perfect that it felt like a dream. We didn't realize just how much we would have to rely on our strong friendship and the sense of awe at what God had done in our lives to carry us through the days to come.

We decided to spend the first night of our honeymoon at my apartment, since it was still paid for until the end of the month. The idea that we were hiding out, practically in our own neighborhood, and nobody knew where we were was kind of amusing and helped take the edge off the nervousness I was feeling. We had made out and played around a lot since our "talk", but this was our first time of going "all the way." My pornographic past had not exactly prepared me to be suave and debonair in seducing my new wife, and that made me a bit apprehensive, but we ended up having a great time, just the same. It felt so good just to have someone to snuggle up with once again.

The next morning, after a leisurely breakfast, we left for a few days in Victoria, B.C. The 90-minute ferry ride to Vancouver Island was gorgeous and we were so happy to be together. We couldn't stop talking about how meaningful the ceremony had been, how lucky we were to have found each other and what a great life was ahead of us.

The Bed and Breakfast we had reserved was even better than their website had promised. It was a beautiful old home, with a private guesthouse out in the garden that was all ours for the weekend. It was an absolutely magical setting for an absolutely magical occasion. After we settled in we headed out to spend the afternoon exploring the museums and shops of Victoria. It was such a wonderful day. After dinner we made our way back to our little cottage and looked forward to spending some romantic time together. We lit the candles we had brought, put on some music and nibbled on the remains of our high tea feast. It was warm and cozy and safe.

Eventually we started kissing. We moved to the bed and things started to heat up. It felt so good. And then, as things progressed, I felt myself starting to shut down just like the old days. I fought against it, but soon I was just going through motions, reacting biologically, and grabbing for fantasies to even accomplish that. Unlike the night before, it felt awkward and empty.

I don't know if it was because I had lofty expectations of what making love should be like in this romantic setting or what, but for some reason things had changed and I was devastated. I really thought that my sexual healing had been completed and now I realized I still had a lot more work to do in that area. "It" was still there and it kept me from being able to stay present with Janet and even worse, it was obvious that she could sense it. It broke my heart when my beautiful wife asked me if I was struggling because she wasn't pretty enough or sexy enough. What should have been a beautiful, romantic evening ended in sadness and tears for both of us We held on to each other desperately until we fell asleep, each of us lost in our own pain and disappointment.

During the rest of our stay we enjoyed the sight-seeing and shopping, but sex continued to be a struggle. I was so upset—and so scared. I was petrified that Janet would reject me now that we had discovered I wasn't as healed as I thought I was. And, of course, the more frightened I got, the more emotionally shut down I became and the worse it was.

Even more disappointments were in store for us once we got back home. It was much harder to adjust to living together than we expected. We kept pushing each other's old buttons—buttons that we didn't even know existed. Something quite innocent would be said and, without even knowing how we got there, things would escalate and one of us would end up being angry, shut down or hurt.

Every time we argued, my fear of abandonment would intensify. If Janet would even start to raise her voice I would experience gripping panic inside me. When I was growing up, bad things happened when anyone got angry and here, years later, I still fully expected that same outcome.

The fact that we were arguing was stressful enough, but when Janet would tell me she "needed space" and wanted to be alone for awhile, which she often did during those first few months, my fears would compound. Spending quality time together was my love language[17]. I always felt the most secure and satisfied with the relationship when we were sharing activities or conversation together in a context that was warm and uninterrupted. The very idea that she wanted or needed time without me made me feel like I wasn't good enough and our relationship was in danger. Even though we had been able to talk about virtually everything before we got married, I couldn't seem to discuss these feelings with her. I felt like there was too much on the line now to risk rocking the boat.

One February Saturday was particularly scary. It was about six months into our marriage and Janet had been bugging me to find something to keep myself busy. She said she had a huge to-do list for the day and thought she'd get more accomplished if she had some time to herself. At her urging I finally decided to go to the rifle range and do some target shooting. I hadn't gone in a very long time, so it would have been fun, if it hadn't felt like I was being pushed out of the house.

When I'd had enough of shooting, I decided to stop by Barnes and Noble to kill a little more time. While I was there, my cell phone rang. I fumbled to get it out of my pocket before it stopped ringing, and as I quickly hit the button, I saw the call was from Janet.

"Hi, kiddo. What's up?"

"I'm really sorry, I just opened your bank statement by mistake. I didn't mean to snoop, but I thought it was our joint account. Before I realized I had the wrong one, I noticed that you've withdrawn a lot of money from your savings account this month. I'm probably being nosy again . . . but what in the world did you buy that cost that much?"

"I'll be right home. We need to talk."

I quickly hung up the phone and tore home. I was dreading what I knew was about to unfold. By the time I walked in our back door, my mouth was bone dry, and I was shaking inside. Even in our worst moments I had always tried to protect my wife from being hurt by anyone or anything, and now, I was the one that was going to inflict profound pain on her. I hated myself for it.

I had really messed things up. A lot of stuff had been getting to me lately: our marriage had been feeling shaky, some changes at work had made it a miserable place to be, and, worst of all, I felt alienated from my kids. I had hoped that now that I had a real home for them to come to, our relationship would improve, but if anything, it had gotten worse. They hadn't embraced Janet as I had expected—they hadn't even given her a chance. Even though they had both come to the wedding, they now seemed angry that I had gotten remarried, and had all but shut me out of their world. It hurt a lot. My life had been feeling more and more out of control and, in spite of everything I had learned, I'd gone back to the one thing that had always helped me get rid of bad feelings before—pornography.

I hadn't been anywhere near the stuff since before we were married, but during the past month, when things felt like they were crashing down around me, I had started buying magazines and renting videos once again.

It wasn't hard for me to find the opportunity to act out. I was working only a few blocks away from home at this point. I was close enough to come home for lunch and with a schedule that included a lot of outreach and a number of evening groups, I had plenty of other time off during the day while Janet was at work, as well.

I couldn't believe how quickly the addiction got back out of control once I started. At first, I had just intended to buy one magazine to help me through a rough spot. But one magazine quickly turned into two, then three, then four. In a matter of days I was acting out every chance I got and, with a need for something new every time, I accumulated 40 or 50 magazines in no time at all.

I felt so guilty every time I brought pornography into the house and I felt just horrible about keeping secrets from my wife. But I just kept doing it. As unbelievable as it seemed, I had spent over $500 on pornography in less than a month. And now it was time to come clean with my wife about it.

It didn't go well.

I think it would have hurt her less if I had thrust a knife into her heart. When I first told her what had been going on she was stunned—like the wind had been knocked out of her. Then she lost it. She sobbed and yelled and sobbed some more. It was even worse than I had expected. I really wasn't sure whether we were going to stay together or not.

One minute she was berating herself for being stupid and making another bad marriage choice and the next minute she was telling me she refused to live like this and that I needed to move out. She said she'd help me find a place to go.

I didn't know what to say. I knew I'd screwed up, and I didn't know how to fix it. I was afraid of her anger and yet, I felt guilty about what I had done to bring it on. I didn't want to lose her, but I felt my emotions shutting down again. I just sat there like I was numb or something. My silence made Janet even crazier.

"Don't you have anything to say? I can't believe you don't even care that our marriage is over. Aren't you even going to try to fight for us? Don't you at least have some regrets? I can't believe you're just sitting there saying nothing."

"I don't want to move out."

"You expect me to just ignore this—to just pretend like it didn't happen? $500 is a lot of money. We can't afford that. I don't want

to always be wondering whether you're out blowing the money we've worked so hard for. I can't live with knowing I'm not good enough or sexy enough for you and you have to go out and find someone or something else to get turned on. It hurts too much. I just can't do it."

"Can we at least pray about it?"

"I suppose that couldn't hurt . . . but I don't really expect it's going to change anything. I'm not even sure you really care. I tell you our marriage is over and you don't cry or get upset or anything. It's like our marriage is no big deal."

"That's not true."

Janet went upstairs and I went to the Living Room to try to get in touch with God. After a lengthy time of praying and reading my Bible, I finally broke down. I didn't want to lose Janet. I didn't want to end our marriage. I needed to go ask her to reconsider. At the same time I heard her coming down the stairs. We met in the front hallway.

"God told me we're supposed to stay together," she said.

"Yeah, I felt like he was telling me the same thing—it's not time to give up. I don't know what to do now, but if He wants us to be together, I guess he'll have to show us that too."

And He did show us. . . little by little . . .bit by bit. We didn't have a clue how to rebuild our relationship, so the only thing we could do was to run to God to show us what to do every time we got stuck or one of us started to feel scared or angry

The next day after church, we agreed that we needed to get rid of the pornography, before we did anything else. We didn't want to risk somebody finding it, like I had done so many years before, so we decided to burn it. We prayed that God would protect our minds from the images as we tore the magazines up and fed them into the fire

Even though the fire was hot, the glossy photos were slow to burn. As we sat in front of the fireplace stirring the fire with the poker, page after page after page curled and disappeared into the flames. It took most of the afternoon to reduce the two large garbage bags of pornography I'd been hiding behind the seat in my truck to a pile of smoldering ashes.

NOW CHOOSE LIFE!

As we neared the end of the last bag, I went to make us a cup of tea. By the time I came back into the room Janet was tearing up the final magazine. I sat down on a footstool next to her. As she threw the last pages into the flames she broke down in wrenching sobs. I leaned down and put my arms around her and held her as she cried and cried. Her sobs seemed to come from someplace deep within her. I'd never heard her cry like that. When she finally calmed down, we prayed for God to show us where to go from here.

Almost immediately, Janet said she was seeing a picture in her head of a clearing in the woods. She told me we were on a path leading into the clearing and I was a little ways ahead of her. As I stepped into the opening, a bear barreled out of the woods toward me. When he began to attack me, she was frantic. She said she was yelling and trying to scare the bear away. Then she noticed that Jesus was standing next to her. She pleaded with him to do something to stop the bear. Jesus just turned toward her and looked at her calmly. She said she was so upset that Jesus wouldn't do anything.

After she told me about what she was seeing she said she had the feeling that I needed to be the one to ask Jesus to save me. I did, and then she saw angels descending on the clearing. As they touched the ground, the bear just turned and sauntered away and the angels began to bandage my wounds.

The vision was very moving for both of us. It confirmed to us that God was, indeed, with us. Interestingly enough, Janet didn't know that I had had nightmares about bears my whole life. The scary bear dreams have never returned after that night.

It had been difficult for me to see how huge the mound of magazines had been. It was an undeniable sign of how out of control I had gotten. It was a mound that had nearly buried my marriage. It wasn't going to be easy to bridge the chasm between us. It would take a long time and a lot of prayer and talking to overcome the awkwardness—the polite and guarded distance—that kept us from reclaiming the special connection we had once had.

Janet . . .

Bruce's difficulties on our honeymoon made me feel inadequate both as a wife and a lover. He was so distraught, that everything in me wanted to do something to "make it better." I wanted him to be OK, but yet I wasn't even feeling very OK myself. I was worried that there was something wrong with ME. If I had been "good enough", maybe he wouldn't be struggling the way he was.

I couldn't figure out why, or what my part in it was, but when we were having sex it didn't feel like Bruce was really with me. I couldn't seem to connect with him. He didn't look at me. He didn't talk to me. It was like he was on some sort of autopilot sprinting toward the finish line. Our honeymoon was my first introduction to Bruce's "robot." When we were "just playing around" it was warm and enjoyable, but if we moved toward intercourse, things always changed. Sex with the robot always left me feeling empty and alone.

Our unexpected difficulties in the bedroom created a dark cloud that hung over every aspect of our marriage. We still talked and enjoyed each other's company, but there was always this huge "but" looming over our relationship. We loved each other . . . but. We had a special relationship . . . but. We were happy . . . but.

Bruce wasn't the only one that was getting his long-dormant buttons pushed and brought back to the surface during that first year of our marriage. I too, was feeling doubts and frustration.

I had known from the time we met that Bruce was more of a "goer" and I was more of a "doer." Even though I had completely enjoyed all the activities and adventures that we had had as friends, it had been a conscious stretch for me to spend so much time socializing. I thought it would be good and healthy (which it was) to strike a better balance between going and doing.

Later, as our relationship progressed, I worried whether I had misrepresented myself as a more social person than I really was. Maybe I had unfairly misled him. I was just as happy—sometimes happier—staying home and cleaning out a closet or working on a remodeling project than running to this event or that. I had always gotten a lot of satisfaction out of accomplishing things. In fact, some might say I was a recovering workaholic.

I, like Bruce, had seen positive changes in that unbalanced part of my life, which led me to believe that I, too, had been healed of those past ways of coping. It wasn't that we were intentionally defrauding each other —we had both sincerely changed from what we used to be, but total healing from anything is a process that often involves numerous layers and an extended period of time. It is rarely simple and instantaneous. Certain issues, like developing healthy sexuality or finding a good social/solo balance are dealt with most effectively within the context of a close relationship with another person. Bruce and I may have gone about as far as we could in those areas as singles. We were at a point where we actually needed someone to "push our buttons" and show us where we still needed work.

Neither one of us understood that concept at first. We truly believed that we had lost something special when our still-broken-areas started to be bumped in a way that we had avoided as singles who could retreat to their own private worlds at the end of the evening. We were afraid that the conflict that came out of learning to operate together 24/7 indicated that there was something wrong with us as a couple. It surprised us when, about this time, a speaker at church[18] posed the question "What if God designed marriage to make us Holy more than to make us happy?" That sermon helped us realize that having our buttons pushed might actually be part of God's divine plan to move us along in our healing journey.

Even though knowledge may help us understand what's going on, it may not make it any easier to navigate through the challenges. Since I was already feeling inadequate, every time Bruce expressed a desire to get away for the weekend, go out to dinner or just kick back on a Saturday that I had already mentally slated for a project, I was sure that his underlying message to me was that the way I did life was unacceptable—he wanted something different. I was sure he was really saying "you're not as good as my first wife" "I'm disappointed in you" "I don't think much of your priorities" Of course he wasn't really saying any of those things, but my internal fears twisted his words as much as his internal fears twisted mine.

It is interesting that, in spite of all my fears and trust issues, when I was actually looking at all the withdrawals on Bruce's bank statement, my mind didn't want to accept the face value of something negative either. Even though my first reaction was gripping panic, I, like many wives that discover their husband's secret activities, initially tried to talk myself out of what I was seeing and feeling. There had to be another explanation. Maybe Bruce had bought me a really special Valentine present with the money. Maybe I was just forgetting about a truck repair bill or some purchase we'd discussed. Most likely I was making a big deal out of nothing. But, in spite of what I tried to tell myself, the lump in my stomach remained. I couldn't shake the cold sweats. I couldn't sit still. I paced. I fretted. As hard as I tried to let it go, something within me KNEW that this was not good.

When I did finally break down and call him, his curt response did nothing to soothe my worries. It took him less than 15 minutes to get home after we talked, but it was the longest 15 minutes in my life. Once he had told me the truth, I was pummeled by an odd mix of intense emotions. . . anger. . . fear. . . betrayal. . . rejection. . . disgust. . . guilt. . .jealousy. . .depression. . . powerlessness. . . confusion. I didn't know what to feel, or if I should be feeling any of it.

As Christians, we sometimes believe we have no right to entertain many of the emotions that well up inside us. We have heard so often that we must "turn the other cheek", "walk the second mile", and "forgive those that harm us" that we refuse to admit any feelings that would seem to be contrary to those directives.

It was popular thinking for a very long time, that we must just "buck up and move on", forget the past and "get over it" . . . but the only way to get over something is to look at it and feel it. In the book of Psalms, David gives us example after example of how to do this. He cries out to the Lord in his anguish and anger and, as he pours out his feelings, he moves toward understanding and gratitude. Once we own and express our feelings to God, the intensity of them goes away. We find ourselves forgiving and going the second mile, but it isn't forced, it is honestly what comes out of our heart.

If we choose, instead, to disregard and deny the things we are experiencing, a very volatile situation is created. Ignored feelings do not go away, instead they fester deep inside until they either begin to eat away at us through physical sickness or self-hatred, or they turn into deep-rooted anger and bitterness that will find external release where and when we least expect it.

At that point in my life, I wasn't very good at processing my feelings. In my fear and confusion, I really could see no other way to get past Bruce's relapse but for us to divorce. It wasn't that I didn't love Bruce. If we had severed our relationship, I truly would have lost my best friend and supporter. Even during our roughest times, our relationship was special. I was just so afraid. . .afraid of looking stupid. . ..afraid of making another mistake. . . afraid that my "man-picker" was still broken. . . and most of all, afraid that I would never be able to trust my husband ever again.

I didn't want to be relegated to the role of mother or warden, continually watching whether he was "behaving" or not. I didn't want to be scared and suspicious all the time. I wanted nothing less than the deep and transparent relationship that we used to have, where we nurtured and supported one another, gave each other courage when we were afraid, and honored God's work in our lives. That, however, seemed lost to us forever, now.

I was surprised when God so quickly changed my thinking about having Bruce leave. Continuing on in the marriage was a scary proposition, but it scared me even more to say no to God. Even knowing without a doubt that God wanted us to stay together didn't automatically take away all my doubts. I definitely had to make a cognitive choice to obey God instead of going with my fears. God acknowledged my apprehension and, over the next few days, gave us several confirmations that we were hearing his voice, including the vision that I saw.

Those who are more conservative might be put off by all the talk about seeing a vision. I want to assure you that I am NOT a "vision" person—in fact, I'm anything but. I'm not attracted to supernatural or eerie things in the least bit. In fact, I normally go way out of my way to avoid them.

I remember Bruce being shocked once when I told him I'd never seen a shooting star. I explained to him that I'd always been too afraid to look up at night—I didn't want to risk seeing a UFO or other strange phenomenon. Even though I am well aware that it seldom works that way, deep down I yearn for life to be fully explainable.

Although seeing these pictures in my head was not logical or explainable, it was very real and undeniable. It felt a lot like I was having a dream while I was awake. I don't fully understand what happened on a spiritual level, but I do know that something radically changed for Bruce that day—it seemed like God moved him another giant step forward in his healing. To this day he has never had another major out-of-control binge like that again. I believe God chose to use the bear symbolism that was significant to Bruce and unknown to me to help convince my doubting brain that He was, indeed, the author of the vision.

24

Preparing to Take Back Our Men

God Begins to Reveal His Plan

Bruce . . .
Ever since the early years of my recovery I had sensed a calling on my life to do some sort of recovery ministry. I had become a chemical dependency counselor, I had facilitated small discussion groups in Living Waters, I had taught Sunday School classes, but I still felt like there was something more that God wanted me to do—I just couldn't quite put my finger on what it was.

Even through the ups and downs of my own healing, the words of 2 Corinthians 1:3-4 stuck with me:

> *"Praise be to the God and Father of our Lord Jesus Christ, the Father of compassion and the God of all comfort, who comforts us in all our troubles, so that we can comfort those in any trouble with comfort we ourselves received from God."*

God and so many people had been there for me over the years, it seemed only right that I should turn around and help someone else find their way. The enemy tried to discourage me by whispering things like "Who are you to try to help anyone when you still have slips yourself?" and "You certainly don't have your act together—what do you have to offer them?", but I was usually able to shrug off those taunts, since my Living Waters experiences had shown me that you didn't have to be completely healed or know everything to help other people in their healing process.

Once I got my feet back on solid ground after my $500 binge, the urge to share what I had received seemed to be reawakened. Janet and I talked about it off and on, but we certainly didn't realize that God was about to send us on a two-year scavenger hunt to gather the tools we needed to do the work he was calling us to do. Those years became a time of change, growth, and excitement for both of us. We didn't know where God was leading us, or how it was all going to work out, but we definitely knew He was preparing us for something.

Desert Stream Ministries, the creator of Living Waters, had been talking for nearly two years about a new program they were developing to address the growing sexual addiction problem. Janet and I could hardly wait to attend the summer leadership conference where they were going to introduce the program and provide training on how to start a group. We were sure that THIS WAS IT! THIS must be what God wanted us to be doing!

The teaching was spiritually inspiring, the newly printed workbook was attractive and informative and, by the time we had been through several days of intensive training, we were chomping at the bit to get home and get started, but . . . God had something else to show us.

After the training, we still had one more day before we were scheduled to fly home. We scanned the list of teaching sessions for the day and were intrigued by a class called "Listening Prayer." Both Janet and I felt like prayer was the weak link in our personal spiritual disciplines, so we hoped that the class would give us a few tips on how to be more effective in our prayers. We never expected, however, that it would be an experience that would literally change our lives.

For the whole three-hour class we sat mesmerized by the speaker. We were absolutely fascinated by his stories and experiences of having two-way conversations with God. What's more, he said that we could ALL have that same sort of relationship with our creator. The words he spoke resonated as truth. Why hadn't we heard this before? We had been Christians for years. It seemed so basic, but yet new at the same time. We got excited about the potential of what he was sharing, bought his book and tapes and resolved to integrate Listening Prayer into our lives the minute we got home.

Unfortunately . . . as with many resolutions, it didn't quite work out that way. When we unpacked our suitcases, we put the books and tapes on the shelf and didn't pick them up again for nine whole months. Once in a while one or the other of us would mention that we really should take another look at the material, but we just never seemed to get around to it.

After months of procrastination, we finally decided to rent a rustic little cabin up by Mt. Baker for the weekend where we wouldn't be distracted by the interruptions of daily life, take our book and tapes up there and see what God wanted to say to us. At first it was scary. It seemed kind of mystical and we weren't sure we would be able to hear anything, but just as the teacher had told us, we eventually started to be able to recognize God's voice. Over the years God has given us so many answers and understandings about everything from the stuck places in my own recovery to the general difficulties of balancing life and ministry. It has changed our image of God and strengthened our relationship with both Him and each other.

We had thought we were going to California to find a program for sexual addiction, but instead, we found a deeper walk with God. The material Desert Stream had developed was full of spiritual truth, but when I tried to work through it, I found myself wishing for more practical instruction on how to apply this Christ-centered teaching to my struggle. It just didn't seem to match my best processing style and I knew that if I couldn't bridge that gap personally, I would have a difficult time helping someone else with it. I was disappointed, but God kept telling us to be patient and that he would point the way one step at a time. Patience—it sure is hard to muster when you're rarin' to go. We knew that people were struggling all around us, and we were frustrated that God wasn't even letting us out of the starting blocks.

NOW CHOOSE LIFE!

In the fall, Karolyn finished the paperwork to create Change of Heart, a non-denominational non-profit recovery ministry. She felt that if the healing ministry was not affiliated with any particular church we would be able to better serve the needs of the entire Christian community. Almost from the start, Janet began to take one day off from her marketing job to work for Change of Heart as we labored to expand our programs and get the word out about what the ministry could offer people.

It was through Change of Heart that we received information on a big conference that was going to be held in Seattle in mid-summer. The sponsors of the event had a successful sexual addiction recovery ministry and wanted to train other people from across the country about how to start a similar program in their vicinity. The minute we read the brochure, we figured THIS WAS IT! THIS must be the program God wanted us to be doing, so we quickly signed up for the four-day conference. Maybe our wait was almost over.

The night before we left, Janet and I took a little break from our packing to ask God what he wanted to tell us about the conference. We were a bit confused by His answers to us:

> *In listening prayer, I heard: "Go in peace with me alongside you. Remember that the people running the conference have brokenness too. Listen and let me discern what you need to hear and take back to your ministry. Good will come from this if you let me be your teacher, counselor and guide. They are doing my work also. Their flaws are not your concern. Let me take care of that. Lighten up and let me show you joy. It does not need to be all work. This is an adventure."*
>
> *Janet heard similar cautions: "My ways are a mystery. Open your ears. Open your hearts. You will hear my voice in the midst of the other voices. I have plans to give you some of what you need from this*

> *conference. The rest will be chaff that drops to the ground and is trampled underfoot. Listen and seek me—I will show you what's important. These are my servants. They are not perfect. Neither will you be. Draw near to me. . . I am the truth."*

We had no idea what God was telling us. It didn't make sense. It seemed like a new door was opening, and we were getting warnings. It seemed very strange to us.

The first night at the conference we got caught up in the excitement of what we were hearing. They seemed to really understand addiction. They defined it well and spoke of the phenomenal success rate of their programs. At the end of the session we went back to our hotel room chattering a mile a minute. We could hardly wait to hear more about how they were doing it at the next morning's session.

Throughout the second day, however, we were growing increasingly frustrated and discouraged. It was becoming more and more obvious that their program didn't even come close to aligning with our personal recovery beliefs. We were convinced that spouses could be an important part of an addict's support system, whereas they believed that it was better if they had no involvement in the healing process at all. We also felt that some of the elements of their program were legalistic, shaming and punitive. It was working for some people, but it certainly didn't fit with who we were or the philosophy of the ministry we represented.

The conference did, however had an impressive line-up of other speakers: Mark & Deb Laaser, Ted & Diane Roberts, Harry Schaumburg, Roy K., Patrick & Marsha Means. Each of them had established ministries to sexual addicts and, I think, all of them had written books. Janet and I spent nearly $200 at the book table, grabbing everything we could on the subject. It was amazing to have all these experts in one place and to be able to hear their experiences. What an opportunity!

The very last speaker of the very last day was Michael Dye, an addiction counselor out of California. We had never even heard of him before, but we were totally fascinated by what he said about "why we do what we don't want to do" and how brain chemistry plays into addictive behaviors. At the end of the hour and a half talk we were hungry to learn more about the things he talked about, so we bought the workbook for the intensive program he had developed called The Genesis Process. Even though the program was originally created to help alcoholics and drug addicts, he assured us that it was applicable to any addictive behavior. When we got home we ordered several of the other books that Michael had mentioned he had found helpful in his research. Everything we read made so much sense and helped me understand what I had experienced in my life and why recovery had been so difficult and long. The concepts opened up a whole new world in relapse prevention.

Once again, we thought we were going for one thing, but left with a totally different tool. But, we weren't done yet. God still had more he wanted us to know . . .

Karolyn and several of the leaders from Change of Heart were making plans to go to the STEPS recovery conference in Porter Ranch, California the following summer. The conference was going to cover recovery of all types, but we were interested to see that several of the speakers we had heard at the conference in Seattle would be speaking about sexual addiction at this conference, as well. Since we were starting to counsel a few sex addicts that had popped up out of nowhere, we were hungry for more training and insight. We were particularly excited to note that Michael Dye would be presenting a full day workshop entitled "Genesis Tools: Understanding and Preventing Relapse" the day before the Steps conference was to begin. After the little taste we had heard before, and our own studying of the workbook we had bought, we were convinced that, even though we had been using all our vacation time for recovery events in recent years we just HAD to go to this one more. All the speakers were good . . . but instead of satisfying us as we thought it would, the day with Michael Dye left us wanting to hear even more.

Every evening after the teaching sessions, there was a mini recovery fair. Some of the speakers and a few other organizations had tables where they sold books, distributed literature and told more about their programs. We stopped by Michael's table one evening to tell him how much we had enjoyed his talk, and how it had left us wanting more. He quickly grabbed a brochure off his table and started telling us about an upcoming Genesis counselor training that was going to be held in Portland Oregon in less than two months.

We assured him that we DID hope to attend one of his training sessions one day, but there was no way we could get time off work and pull the $450 tuition money for each us together in just a few months. He said if there was any way we could work it out to attend this session we should—it was a one-time opportunity to get room and board for the week for just $25 a person. Evidently the Portland Rescue Mission had just completed a top-notch long-term residential facility to house Shepherd's Door, their ministry to women and children. Since it had only just opened and was only partially filled, they had invited Michael to do his next counselor training there. Instead of the normal hotel costs, and expensive meals . . . we could get brand new rooms and three hearty meals for just $5 a day. It was tempting . . . but unrealistic. We both worked for small companies and had just taken a week off work. There was no way we would be able to get more time off so soon. Michael didn't give up easy though— he insisted we take a brochure "just in case."

As unlikely as it was, neither one of us could quite let go of the idea of attending that training. We wanted to hear more. But there was no way. We finally decided that we'd pray about it and even go so far as to ask at work, but we both assumed the answer would be a resounding no. We were flabbergasted when we approached our bosses and they said "no problem." It was so out of character for both of them. So . . . that's how, just hours after getting home, we found ourselves making travel arrangements for the next venue of this "gathering mission" God had us on.

The new facility in Portland was phenomenal. The rooms were nice (except that we had to sleep in twin beds) and the food was wonderful. The cooks were using this as a practice run for cooking for large crowds and they did a bang-up job. There were at least 50 people attending the training, in addition to the 20 or so moms and children that were some of the first to be accepted into Portland Rescue Mission's innovative women's shelter program.

As Janet and I sat in the sunny classroom the first day, we were still amazed at how God had gotten us there. The other participants were from all over the country. Some of them already worked in the rescue mission setting, some were pastors wanting to add this type of recovery program to their church's schedule, and still others, like us, were hoping to use the material in another way, to reach a different group of people.

It was a tough week. In addition to the training sessions, we were each required to personally go through the entire 10-Process program during the week. Every night we would go back to our rooms to complete our self-reflective homework. Every day we had six or seven hours of class time and one-on-one processing with the people we were teamed up with. Most evenings Michael Dye would also facilitate an additional optional informal session where we could get questions answered and watch how he used some of the tools and prayer techniques in an actual counseling session.

It was a very full and exhausting time, but it was also extremely exciting. Every session resonated with us and explained so much of what I'd seen and experienced. It was refreshing to see a program that focused on the underlying needs of the person as a whole instead of just their problematic behavior. Along with solid Bible-based teaching, it provided practical exercises designed to help a person discover what keeps them from being able to change their unwanted behaviors. Every aspect of the program imparted an abundant measure of grace, hope and truth.

After a journey that included two trips to California, a trip to Oregon and several jaunts around Washington State, we felt confident that we had finally assembled the tools that would become the foundation of our sexual addiction recovery program. Of equal importance, was the fact that God had led us to tools that would be essential in the next phase of my own ongoing recovery.

Janet . . .

One day in Listening Prayer, God described the ministry he was preparing us for as "going into the battlefield to take back our men." Considering how much the enemy seems to be using sexual addiction to ruin lives and families in today's society, it seemed like a fitting picture of what needed to be done—to go behind enemy lines and free the captives.

Ever since we'd brought home a bulging suitcase full of books from the Seattle conference I'd been reading and reading and reading. I had read everything I could get my hands on about sexual addiction and other related topics. I'm a researcher at heart and I enjoy pulling bits and pieces together and seeing how they relate and interact. Bruce, on the other hand, does his best processing verbally. In sharing what I was reading and discussing it with Bruce, God used both of our natural gifts and tendencies to help us develop supplementary materials to aid in explaining difficult concepts.

Some books brought "ah-ha moments" that deepened our understanding, others made us angry at their unfair portrayal of those struggling with this addiction or the lack of hope that they provided. God seemed to shine a light on other random thoughts as if he was saying "take note of this . . . it's important" and eventually that small piece would fit with the pieces from other sources to provide new ways to illustrate and present God's truth.

Some of the most exciting books we studied were those on the brain. We had first heard about the connection between the brain and addiction from Michael Dye. In the past decade, significant research has been done in relation to the brain. Using sophisticated brain scan technology, scientists are able to actually see the parts of the brain that become active in response to various situations and track the firing sequences in the brain. This is bringing us much closer to understanding what happens physiologically in response to fears and feelings.

The Limbic System is the part of the brain that controls both the emotions and the body's automatic survival responses. It is interesting that it is found deep in the core of the brain, where it is least vulnerable to injury. Its very location and function is an indication of how much God wants us to survive. When we are in a state of anxiety or fear, the limbic system acts independently from our conscious minds to tell us to fight, run, or freeze—whatever is required to keep us safe from impending or perceived danger. Every single awareness that we take in through our senses—seeing, hearing, touching, smelling or tasting—goes first to the limbic part of the brain so it can be flagged as safe or dangerous.

Unlike the cognitive thinking part of our brain that continues to develop well into our early 20s, the Limbic System is fully developed and fully functional when we are born. Right from our first day on earth (and probably before), it begins "learning" what is and is not safe through our life experiences.

The first time, as a toddler, that we touch a stove and burn ourselves, the limbic system stores the idea that hot stoves are a danger to our well-being. After that, our brain automatically, without us even being aware of it, sends a message to our hand to pull away each time we encounter a hot stove to help us avoid further pain and keep ourselves safe.

The same sort of programming happens in response to emotional pain, as well. Bruce's limbic system had quickly learned to associate his mother's anger and rage with the danger of rejection and isolation. Subsequently, any inkling of anger, especially in women, instantly put Bruce's brain in danger awareness mode and sent him looking for a way to avoid what it believed was inevitable pain. Even though, in most cases, the danger was non-existent, his brain falsely believed that anger always led to rejection and continued to do so, until new experiences in recovery revised the danger factor of anger. Unfortunately, because we have learned to automatically respond by fighting, fleeing or freezing when faced with a situation that seems scary and dangerous, we often find it difficult, if not impossible, to allow ourselves the opportunity to experience anything different and we end up very, very stuck.

Everyone has their way or ways of avoiding pain. Some will automatically fight back. Fighting may manifest itself in obvious ways like yelling, arguing or blaming, or it may show itself in more subtle actions, like trying harder, workaholism, perfectionism or people pleasing, all of which are intended to send an "oh, yeah . . . I'll show you" message. Even sarcasm and gossip can sometimes be used as a more passive–aggressive way of fighting back.

Fleeing, or "flight" may involve actually physically running away and isolating, or it may be achieved by simply shutting down emotionally or dissociating mentally from the situation. Many people use drugs, alcohol or even sexual behaviors to help them shut down and numb unwanted feelings.

Still others may believe that they are incapable of fighting or running, so they just freeze. They, too, may become emotionally numb, or they may find themselves getting sick or depressed. Others just give up and develop a sort of learned helplessness that keeps them from trying to find a way out of their stuckness. In essence, they just roll up in a ball until the storm passes.

When faced with a situation or fear that feels familiar, the Limbic System is what creates a craving for the fight/flight/freeze activity that has helped us survive in the past. Consistently giving into those cravings produces a compulsive behavior and, as we become more and more reliant on that compulsion to keep us feeling OK, it can quickly develop into an addiction.

Because of this, permanently stopping an addiction by trying to stop a behavior is nearly impossible. Short-term success may be seen, but only until the Limbic System once again senses danger and sends out a craving for the trusted behavior. The only sure way to gain complete freedom is by letting Jesus rewrite the false beliefs that trigger our fears and subsequently sends our limbic system into overdrive.

25

Rocky Roads and Thoroughfares

Rough Times and New Revelations as a Couple

Bruce . . .
About a year and a half after my infamous $500 binge, I started having serious cravings to act out again. Thoughts and temptations had surfaced from time to time throughout those many months, but until now I had always been able to resist them. This time was harder. The mental images and fantasies seemed unrelenting. It took almost nothing to send me down that wayward path.

My work situation, that had been so difficult before, had deteriorated to the point that it was barely tolerable. I was working long hours; my boss was demanding more and more and giving the employees less and less in the way of support or encouragement; my client load was well beyond what anyone could realistically accommodate; and I was on the edge of emotional burn-out.

On top of that, in what little free time we had, Janet and I had been trying unsuccessfully to get the sexual addiction ministry off the ground. By this time we'd already been to the Living Waters and Seattle conferences, but could not yet see that God was actually in the process of developing—bit by bit; conference by conference— the program he wanted us to offer. We were feeling extremely frustrated and let down by all the times we thought we finally "had the answer" only to have it slip through our fingers once again. To be honest, I felt like a victim and a failure in every area of my life.

On this particular day, I was scheduled to do an evening counseling group and didn't have go into the office until noon. Janet was at work, so I'd just been hanging out at home all morning, catatonically flipping through the channels on the TV, and feeling pretty useless. As it got closer to the time that I needed to start getting ready for work, I remember thinking that I just couldn't face making another peanut butter sandwich for lunch. I decided, instead, to hurry and get dressed and stop by Burger King for a hamburger. Looking back, I realize that it was no coincidence that I subconsciously chose to eat at a restaurant that shared its parking area with a sex shop.

While I was sitting in the booth eating my lunch, my gaze kept wandering out the window and across the parking lot. I remember thinking that it was too bad I was on my way to work because a little pornography would be a welcome relief about now. It sure would be great to just dive into it and forget all about work and the ugly things I was feeling about myself—even if it was just for a few minutes. "Boy," I thought to myself, "It's been such a long time since I've bought a magazine. It's not like I'd be going on a binge or anything. I just need something to help me get rid of the yuckiness I'm feeling. I won't go crazy this time. Really, I won't. Just one magazine and then I'll get right back on track again."

I checked my watch. If I hurried I'd still have enough time to pick up a magazine and then I could worry about finding a time to act out later on. I knew exactly what magazine I wanted. It'd only take a few minutes to go in and grab it and then I'd be all set when I did have some time alone. Oh, what the heck . . . I'd be crazy not to go for it. I didn't get many opportunities like this.

I wolfed down the last few bites of my burger, crumpled up the wrapper and tossed it into the garbage on my way out the door. My gait quickened and so did my heart rate as I got closer to the store. Oh, yeah . . . this was exactly what I needed . . . I could hardly wait.

I made a beeline for the magazine rack and quickly scanned the titles until my eyes caught sight of the one I was looking for. I had it in my hand and was headed for the check stand before I even had time to take another breath. As the cashier was ringing up my sale, I glanced at my watch again. Oh, shoot . . . I had to be at work in five minutes. I wouldn't even have time to break the pesky seal the store put on the magazines to keep people from looking without paying, let alone thumb through it. What a raw deal!

As I made my way out to the parking lot I was surprised by the intensity of the anger I was feeling. Even though I'd told myself all along that the magazine was "for later," I was getting increasingly frustrated that I didn't have time to act out right NOW. Spending a little time with that magazine is what I REALLY wanted to do— that's what I "needed."

In spite of my internal battle, I slipped the magazine, sack and all, behind the truck seat and headed off to work. It almost hurt physically to resist taking a peek. It would have felt so good to veg out and hide in it and forget about all the crap that I was dealing with.

My mind kept sneaking back to those glossy pages all day long. I had to force myself to focus on my groups and clients and paperwork. Whenever I had the smallest breather, thoughts of that magazine would once again hijack my brain. I wondered if there was anything exciting in its pages . . . some new ads? . . . reading the personal ads always got me going. . . maybe there was somebody new I hadn't seen before. It had been so long, there could be a bunch of new stuff. Just thinking about the possibilities turned me on.

Minute by minute, I talked myself through the afternoon, "just be patient, Bruce, you'll have time to look at it later . . . maybe even tomorrow." "Quit being so impulsive." "C'mon, you've got to stop obsessing on it. There's nothing you can do about it now."

Time crawled by, but, at last, my evening group was over. Just a half hour more and I was out of there. I tried to concentrate on doing the progress notes for the group. What a pain in the butt! I had never really liked the paperwork part of my job, anyway, and tonight it was even more grueling than usual. I just wasn't in the mood. If it wasn't so darn hard to remember the details later on, I would've thrown it all back in the file cabinet to deal with another day.

It was a huge relief when I was finally able to sign the last page and begin gathering up my stuff. As I locked the door behind me and walked into the nearly vacant parking lot I started wondering whether there would be enough light in our driveway when I got home to at least thumb through the magazine before I went into the house. It might give me something to fantasize about until I could REALLY get into it after Janet left for work in the morning. I was so deep in thought as I came around the back of the truck that it totally took me by surprise to see Karolyn standing near my driver's door.

What was she doing here? She'd never come to my work before. For some reason I didn't put two and two together.

"Hi, Bruce."

"Hi."

"I need to ask you a question," She paused for just a minute and then went on. "Were you at the bookstore today?"

Oh, shit. She knew . . . "Yes,"

"Did you buy anything?"

"Yea, I bought a magazine. Why?"

"Someone saw you and called me. They were worried about you."

I knew I'd never get a chance to see the magazine now. I'd spent the money, and now I'd never even know what was in it. A hollow, knotted feeling settled in my stomach. What a mess! What had I been thinking? I'd done so well for so long. Why today? Why hadn't I been more careful? Karolyn knew. Somebody else knew. And, now I was going to have to go home and tell my wife that I had slipped again. The giddy anticipation that I had left the office with was swallowed up by a torrent of dread.

I was so upset with myself that I could barely hear as Karolyn told me I needed to set up a counseling appointment to talk about what was going on. My head was spinning as she got into her car and drove into the darkness.

I stood stunned for a minute, and then I climbed into the truck. Instead of excitement, I now felt disgusted about the magazine that was wedged behind my seat. The drive home felt like walking up the steps to the gallows.

The house was quiet as I turned the doorknob. I dropped my briefcase by the chair and went to find Janet. The minute I saw her I could tell she knew something was going on.

I found out later that Karolyn had called the house asking to talk to me. When Janet told her I was still at work, she asked what time I got off and quickly hung up as soon as she got her answer. The strangeness of the call set off Janet's radar.

By the time I got home several hours later, she was actually pacing the floor. She didn't know what was going on, but she sensed it wasn't good. She was so angry when I told her the whole story.

It felt like an arrow piercing my chest when she said she didn't know how many more of these episodes she could go through. I knew she wasn't just being dramatic. I knew there was truth in her words. She had always been patient and supportive of my struggle, but she was warning me that there was a limit.

She couldn't believe that I had been willing to risk destroying the ministry we had been working so hard to build. What if it was someone we were trying to help that saw me. I wasn't just hurting myself anymore, I had the potential of hurting a lot of innocent people.

For a fleeting moment I wondered whether my decision to be so open about my addiction and recovery had been such a great idea. In an effort to help others find freedom, I had shared with a lot of people over the years. Janet was right. The consequences of my slips had the potential of reaching far beyond me and my family. It was a sobering thought.

Janet . . .

During the first years of our marriage, Bruce had one or two "slips" each year. Even though the slip usually involved buying a magazine or two and often not even having the opportunity to use them before he was caught, they were still difficult times for both of us and for our marriage. Surprisingly, God always turned these rocky patches into highways that lead to new healing.

The slips did not cause the growth . . . but it was at those times we were most desperate to receive God's wisdom. We were most open. I'm sure that the new awarenesses and healing could have happened without the slips—if we had been able to keep seeking—but we, like so many, had a tendency to get lazy and apathetic when things were going well.

Above all else, we began learning that God wants relationship with us. No matter what we've done; no matter how often we've failed Him; He WANTS to be an integral part of our daily lives. We get it so messed up. We often want to believe that all we need to do is plead and grovel, get healed, and then go on our merry way. We don't realize that it is IN the give and take of an ongoing relationship with God that we find the true healing that we seek—not because our own efforts have earned us a coveted "appointment" with the Great Physician.

The day after Karolyn confronted Bruce at work I was still feeling intense anger and betrayal. Even though my head knew that Bruce's addictive behaviors started long before we ever met, and that his slip had nothing to do with lust or my acceptability as a woman, it was still very difficult to resist the temptation to put myself down and chastise myself for not seeing it coming or helping it to stop.

As the day progressed, my anxiety and negative self-talk became so intense that I finally decided to do some Listening Prayer and see if God would help me understand the situation. Even today, when life starts to close in around me, I often reread God's poignant instruction that I recorded in my prayer journal that day:

> *"Forgive Bruce. He has hurt you in places you did not know could hurt. He has brought an ache to your soul—but he has not taken the joy that you can experience in me.*
>
> *I did not choose this path for him. His wrong choices brought him to the edge of the cliff. But I will not*

let him jump off. I called to him and he looked up to me. He is not alone now—he is holding my hand again. As long as he's willing to do that, I will guide him to the right path—the path of life.

Don't harden your heart to him or to me. I will be the golden cord in your rope. I will be the knot that keeps you from unraveling. If two cords entwined together are stronger than one, think how much stronger the three shall be. Our cord of three cannot be broken, but it will come apart without my knot to secure it.

You made wrong choices as well. His mistakes are not your fault, but you did not do what I have told you. You did not stay close to me and you did not cast your cares on me. I cannot protect either of you if you keep me at arms length. This is a battle. I need to be your shield. I need to become a part of you. I cannot keep you from the fiery darts if I'm not allowed to walk with you. I cannot protect you from across the field.

In this ministry I have chosen for you and you have accepted, you cannot afford the luxury of nonchalance. Periodic visits with me will not be enough to sustain you. Some may be able to do this—although it is never my choice for them—but if you are going into the battlefield; if you are going to help me take back our men—you need to be gird with protection EVERY day. I don't say this to make you feel guilty. I say this because I love you and I know what you're up against.

Don't retreat —but be more diligent in your preparation for battle. This is not a time for carelessness. Lives, both yours and theirs are at stake

> *here. How can I make you see the direness of the situation? How can I make you understand how crucial this is? You cannot go into battle without my protection. The enemy will devour you. I am stronger than he—I will win every battle—but he is very aware of when you are stepping out without me. You are not strong enough or smart enough to win without my help. Truth is truth!"*

Our Christian walk, and our recovery, is a series of choices. Michael Dye, creator of the Genesis Process says "the right thing is usually the hard thing." For both Bruce and I, the hard thing is to "cast our cares on Him." It seems like it would be easy to let go of our burdens . . . but the enemy and our own self-sufficiency continually tell us that we don't need anyone—we can handle things all by ourselves.

For Bruce that drive to isolate and take care of himself—to be his own savior—leads back to addictive behaviors. For me it creates unhealthy levels of stress, worry and drivenness that affect my emotional, physical and even spiritual wellbeing. We NEED that daily relationship with the only one that can truly save us.

Only a few months after receiving this word from God, doors started to open, and we began to lead our first individual clients through the Genesis Process. Just a year later we started our first men's sexual addiction recovery group.

I wish I could say that we'd instantly learned our lesson and never wandered out into the field under our own power again, but only a month after starting that group, I came home a little early from work one day, with a miserable head cold. It was probably only the third or fourth time in my entire work history that I hadn't hung in there and finished the day, sick or not.

As I turned the car into our alley I was surprised to see that Bruce's truck was already parked in our driveway. He should have been at work. I had a sick feeling in my stomach as I got out of the car. As I entered the house and came toward the bedroom, I caught a frantic flurry of activity . . . bare skin . . . pants being yanked up .

. . a magazine being tossed to the ground . . . and the familiar black sack of the adult bookstore laying on the bed.

After nearly a year of no "slips", Bruce had cashed in the money in his coin jar, left early from work with a "headache" and went to several porn stores looking for his favorite Swingers magazine. Not only had he spent nearly $40 of the money he had been saving for a GPS unit, but he had once again risked the ministry and our marriage.

Even though this latest surprise had left me feeling even worse than when I came home, I had an appointment to go to that evening that I couldn't miss. As I left the house, Bruce was just sitting down to begin the back-track exercise that we use with our clients when they have had a slip, and to spend some time listening to God. He asked God to help him understand why he had turned toward his addiction once more. God again reminded him how important it was to stay connected:

> *"It didn't just happen. You've been drifting away from health for a while. You cannot afford to not be connected. The subtle changes have a way of building up. I do not tell you to connect with me just to talk or communicate, but as a way of getting out of your own mind and old patterns that are not bad by themselves, but tend to build up over time. It is like the story of the frogs in the cold water. If you gradually heat up the water they won't realize they're in danger until it's too late.*
>
> *You also need to connect with human beings. Start sharing more with your wife and be on the lookout for others that I will send your way. Again if you are to survive being a leader you cannot allow isolation."*

As Bruce continued to explore the events and feelings of the previous days he began to realize just how disconnected he had allowed himself to become from me, God and others. He also recognized that he had been repeatedly ignoring the obvious signs he was in trouble. By the time I got home, he had already prayed and repented for his choices, but he said he didn't feel like he had found any real resolution. He still felt numb and unemotional about the whole episode.

As we talked we began to wonder why he had gone to such great lengths to find one particular magazine. He was disgusted by the whole idea of "swinging" and yet it was the only magazine that he wanted. Often fantasy themes or sexual preferences are windows to a legitimate need. What was so special about the Swingers magazine? Was he somehow trying to fill an authentic need with the ads from real women flaunting their sexuality?

After a grueling conversation of dead-ends and "theory" answers, that just didn't seem to take us anywhere, Bruce was visibly affected when I asked him, "Aren't these "real" women proving your mother wrong? Aren't they saying, 'see . . . women DO like sex'? Don't they affirm your manhood? They say in their ads that they "want" you. They honor your ability to satisfy them in the ways they ask. They say your sexuality is not only OK, but desired. Isn't that the real need? To know that you, as a sexual being, are acceptable?"

As he struggled to hold back his tears, Bruce admitted that these words felt like truth, but that he had believed almost all of his life that his sexuality was bad. He always felt that in the process of distancing from it, he had permanently destroyed it. Knowing that God was the only one that knew the truth, he returned to Listening Prayer. God not only assured him that it still existed, but he likened it to a valuable jewel:

> *"Open the door that you closed as a child and let me polish the diamond so it can shine. I tried to open your mom's door and she could not listen or hear me. Your precious stone is not gone, only hidden, and when I shine it, it will shine to others."*

Recovery is like peeling an onion. It is a slow process that involves pulling back the layers of brokenness and pain one at a time and bringing God into each issue that comes to the surface. Nothing goes away until it is resolved. Even if we think we have been successful in running away from it or ignoring it, it is still there festering under the surface, until it has been dealt with. God knows, however, that if we had to face every one of our wounds and false beliefs all at once, we would be absolutely overwhelmed by the pain of it. Because of His great love for us, our heavenly Father usually chooses to bring things up one at a time, as we are ready (and willing) to look at them. God used each of Bruce's slips to uncover a significant layer that was still in need of His healing touch.

Over the years, Bruce had become aware that one of the key signs he was in trouble was when he started sexualizing the women around him. When he was doing OK, he saw them simply as friends, co-workers and pretty girls on the street, but when he was heading for relapse, they became "nice butts", "great cleavage" and fodder for all kinds of fantasy.

Even with this understanding, he often still tried to ignore the signs and convince himself that he could handle it alone, without having to tell anyone what was going on. Deep down, though, he was well aware that it was a major indication that he was in danger.

Strangely, he hadn't been experiencing any of that the next time he felt the urge to buy a magazine. He had been to the doctor and was on his way back to the office to prepare for an evening group when he, seemingly out of the blue, took a "detour" by way of the adult bookstore. He stopped, made a purchase, then climbed back into the truck, stuffed it into his briefcase and continued on to work.

By the time his group was over, the building was quiet and everyone seemed to be gone for the day. As he went into his office to finish up his paperwork before heading home, he remembered the magazine he had bought earlier in the day. Since I was working out of our house full-time for Change of Heart by then, I guess he was afraid he might not get an opportunity to use it right away and decided to take a quick peek before he started on his paperwork. Evidently he had barely started thumbing through it when he was startled by someone calling his name. Even though he wasn't doing anything but looking at some of the pictures, his automatic response, as it had been since he was a child, was to panic and try to hide the magazine. His boss, watching all this from the doorway of his office, got suspicious and asked him what he was looking at. Caught in the act, he had little choice but to confess.

When he came home and told me what had happened, I was more scared than ever before. We both knew he could have been fired for such risky behavior while on the job. Thankfully, all his employers did was require him to develop an accountability plan and get some additional counseling.

Unfortunately, their show of grace did little to calm my own deep fears. Even if Bruce did think he was alone, he knew he was taking a chance. My husband had been willing to risk his job—our very livelihood— for a few minutes of looking at pornography. I wasn't sure how much more of this I could —or should—put up with. Our life felt like a house of cards that could come crashing down around us at any time.

Every time Bruce had a slip I felt like we went back to square one as a couple—except square one seemed to keep moving farther and farther away from where we wanted to be living. Each time I found out about another episode, my trust in him would again be crushed and I would have to fight hard to not let anxiety and suspicion get the upper hand. Often I would be afraid to leave him alone, and if I ever arrived home earlier than I expected, panic would grip me as I turned into our alley for fear of, once again, seeing his truck in the driveway when it shouldn't have been, or walking in on him while he was acting out.

It would usually take many months to rebuild the trust and feel like I could relax again. I was tormented by the idea that it might always be like this—the fear; the anxiety; the impending doom of him getting caught and us losing the ministry and the good things we had in our relationship. The trepidation that maybe someday it wouldn't just be a magazine . . . but a massage parlor or a prostitute. This incident at work only added more fuel to my deepest fears but, once again, God's words helped guide me through the difficult times:

> *"Be still my little one. Let me hold you and comfort you. You do not always have to be so strong—melt into me—I will protect you from the storms.*
>
> *Let Bruce work through the consequences of his bad choices. Everything will be OK—better than before.*

He has had much healing—but there are still things he must become aware of to walk away from his old ways for once and for all. He can win this battle. He can live in freedom, if only he will write on his heart and burn into his mind the things I show him.

He must learn to ward off the evil tempter. He has other paths now—paths that will bring him through the wilderness without a scratch—but it takes time to become familiar with the trailhead. The terrain has changed and he must get his bearings—he must establish new landmarks.

Take comfort—he is not avoiding the issues as in times past. The desires he speaks of are real. Give him time, just a little, and he will solidify his way."

And it was true . . . my husband was not avoiding the issues. He dug deep to find out why he had felt the need to return again to his addictive behaviors. We prayed, we talked, we listened to God, both together and separately, and little by little he began to learn new things about himself. Working back through the weeks, Bruce saw a growing pattern of isolation, resentment and helplessness during the previous month. Seeing the opulent new offices his doctor had just moved into, when we were having to pay so much for insurance and health care, brought his mounting anger to a head. It was the final straw that sent him over the edge—looking for something to temporarily make him feel better.

He further realized that the reason he hadn't experienced the normal "sexualizing women" warning sign was actually an indication that he was healthier than he had been in the past. The healing he had received allowed him to actually feel some of the underlying feelings of anger and injustice instead of automatically moving toward the sexual cure. In looking back over many of his past slips, he saw that there was a common thread. Every time he had been feeling like a victim—angry, isolated and helplessness—exactly what he had been feeling just prior to buying this last magazine.

NOW CHOOSE LIFE!

Victim thinking can be such an automatic habit. Bruce and I have often told the story about the time we decided to have a frozen pizza for lunch. Bruce got it out of the freezer and when he opened it up, he saw that all the pepperoni had slid to one side of the pizza. Standing in the middle of the kitchen, pizza in hand, he angrily sputtered, "Look what they've done. The pepperoni is all on one side." I reached over and picked up a piece of pepperoni and said "well then move it." He looked at me with the funniest look.

Later when we were laughing about the pizza incident, Bruce admitted that, even though it was ridiculously obvious the minute he heard it, it had never even entered his mind that he had the freedom to move the pepperoni until I suggested it. In his world he had learned that you are stuck with the hand life deals you and there isn't anything you can do about it—a learned helplessness that kept him feeling like a victim for nearly five decades.

Now that he is aware of how dangerous it is for him to start pulling away from people, building resentments, and feeling like a victim, he has made great strides in learning to resolve the issues that lead to those feelings. He's learned to express his desires and needs, instead of just willingly accepting whatever is shoved on him; he is talking about things that feel unfair before they become resentments and he is continuing to work at reaching out to people instead of isolating when he feels bad or is scared. The more successful he has become at dealing with these core issues, the less he has been haunted by any cravings to act out.

He doesn't always get it 100% perfect. There are still days that I can see mild resentments starting to build or hear the old victim voice gaining strength, but when they do, we've been able to talk about what he's feeling, and he's been able to take steps to free himself from that insidious quicksand before it takes over.

His change in thinking and attitude was particularly obvious a few years ago, when he very unexpectedly lost his job. In the face of the kind of deep rejection and injustice that would have always sent him running directly to the "safety" of pornography in the past, his persistence in spending time in introspection, discussion and prayer, kept him from even being tempted. The most exciting thing is that, every time a person works through something that touches their core issues without going to their old thinking or addictive behaviors, it starts to retrain their limbic system and takes just a little of the power away from the things that used to trigger them. Given enough of those positive experiences, the old triggers will virtually disappear. It no longer takes white knuckling and trying harder to keep from acting out, there is a real and permanent heart change.

I once heard it said,, "Perseverance always takes you into new territory—and you WILL fail—but it is in that failure that you learn how to succeed." In our healing journey, we will often stumble, but instead of lying in the muck or turning back, we need to continually get up, brush ourselves off and turn quickly to God for his guidance, encouragement and wisdom.

26

But Wait . . .
There's More!

Pursuing Healthy Sexuality

Bruce . . .

I always thought that if I could just get enough healing to stop acting out, everything would be OK from then on. I discovered, however, that just slowing or stopping the addictive behaviors is not enough. The second, equally challenging, phase of sexual addiction recovery is developing a healthy sexuality.

In theory, it seems like it should be easy. If you just take away everything unhealthy —you'll be left with healthy, right? Oh, how I wish that were true! All I know is that it certainly hasn't worked that way for me, nor any of the men we've worked with over the years.

First of all, what is healthy sexuality, anyway? I wasn't even sure who to ask, other than God himself. There don't seem to be very many relationships that haven't been impacted by the "Hollywoodization" of our sexuality. Having been steeped for years in a world of especially distorted sexual expressions, I didn't have a clue what "normal" was, and even less idea as to whether what had become normal in our society was actually what God intended it to be.

I remember being extremely frustrated about this one day. I knew there was no way to reach a goal I couldn't even visualize and, to make it even more complicated, I still wasn't totally convinced that my sexuality hadn't been irrevocably broken. When I asked God about his take on it, He said:

> "I made the engine—it is good. Your sexuality is intact and it is good because I made it without blemish. The enemy and incidences in your past have short-circuited the running of it. In your panic you have tried to rewire it. You made it run, but not well. It is not in tune—it runs rough— it is temperamental—you cannot trust its performance. You are missing out on so much because your efforts to repair it were flawed. Let me do it right. I know the parts that need replacing. I know how to make it run smoothly. Stand back and watch as I show you how it needs to be fixed."

I found it humorous that, when God spoke to me, he referred to "the engine." We had often talked to our groups about "stopping the engine." In that context, we were referring to stopping their acting out long enough to feel the pain that fueled their addictive behavior so they could figure out what was broken. Now God was telling me that not only did He make the engine in its unbroken condition, but He knows how to restore it.

I was relieved to hear that my sexuality was not destroyed and intrigued that God wanted to be such an integral part of its redemption. I think, as humans, we often get the idea that our spirit is good; our body is bad. But Christ came to redeem ALL of us— our body, mind and spirit. He wants to return us to our original state— the one God called "good" when he created Adam. He didn't say the spirit was good, the mind was questionable, and the body was trouble. He said His creation—the whole thing—was good.

In my life, however, I had always had a hard time seeing sex as anything good or valuable. Sexuality seemed to be a constant source of hurt and pain for anyone who got near it. Many times I became so repulsed by my sexual behaviors, that I tried to distance myself from

ANYTHING sexual. For all intents and purposes, I became asexual during those periods. It was a nice breather from the bad expressions of sexuality but it was equally devastating to the healthy intimacy God intended for me.

As I became more healed ... I again found myself in that sexually anorexic state. Now it was not because I was trying to escape from anything, but because my true sexuality was virtually undeveloped. It had basically stopped maturing when it was sidelined by the self-satisfaction of pornography and masturbation. Even though my whole life had become focused on sexual pursuits, I didn't have a clue how to be sexual in a healthy way.

It was so frustrating. I adored my wife and yet I couldn't make love to her in a way that felt wholesome, satisfying and intimate for both of us. We were open and transparent in every other area of our marriage. We could share our deepest fears, hopes, and dreams. We could talk about spiritual beliefs and political ideas without concern of being misunderstood or put-down—but we were unable to find the same safe connection physically.

God helped me realize that I would never be able to share my true sexuality with someone else as long as it was a stranger to me. One-by-one I needed to eliminate all the misjudgments, coping skills, and fears I had developed relating to sex and get back to where I, as a terrified 11 year old boy, started down the wrong path because I was convinced I was becoming what I had vowed at age 4 never to be. I didn't realize then that the sexual thoughts and feelings I was experiencing were normal and good and should have been embraced instead of feared.

In some ways I felt like I was being sent on a rescue mission to find the sexuality that a young boy believed he had to hide to be acceptable, and then to allow God to refine and mature it in the way that should have happened naturally as I grew into manhood. It has been a difficult, and often daunting, quest that has necessitated that I let go of many of the things that have helped me feel safe and enabled me to "perform" sexually.

NOW CHOOSE LIFE!

When we are faced with unmet needs and developing false beliefs about ourselves and others, our limbic survival brain may commandeer a part of our true self to help protect us from getting hurt further. These "survival personalities" are not like multiple personalities—they are just facets of ourselves that end up being used for the wrong reason. Just as we might have a "serious side" or a "crazy side" that is predominate in certain settings, we may have survival personalities that have been created to deal with specific challenges or conditions.

Although we may have missed some, Janet and I have become aware that the limbic part of my brain has created at least five self-sufficient survival personalities to get me through a variety of hard times and difficult situations.

The first one, that we call Scared Boy was created at age 3 or 4 to help me deal with an unpredictable, rageful mother and an unsafe family environment. All normal humans have the capacity to be scared. God intended for us to be able to "read" people and situations and to discern when we are in real danger—but he didn't intend for that state to be a 24/7 way of life. My brain decided that being scared could provide a means of protection. Based on my experiences I had decided "it's not safe to be a boy"; "authority figures cannot be trusted", "If someone is angry or yells, someone is going to get hurt", and "anger must be avoided at all cost." Well into my adulthood these false beliefs reigned my life . . . and whenever they were challenged . . . Scared Boy would hunker down and hide. In my youngest days I would hide behind the couch or under the table, later on I hid in the pages of pornography.

When I was about six, Silly Boy was created to deal with a different set of issues. There had always been a lot of fighting in my family. It usually wasn't directed at me, so Scared Boy wasn't alerted to take charge, but it made me uncomfortable, nevertheless.

God had blessed me a good sense of humor that I'm sure He intended would make life more enjoyable and put people at ease. My brain's best thinking, however, told me that I could use it to protect myself from inevitable pain. It assured me that if I made people laugh they'd like me and wouldn't notice when I was feeling angry, scared or vulnerable. I began to believe that it was my job to diffuse the bad situations before they got out of hand. So . . . whenever there was tension and fighting in my family, the survival part of my brain would summon Silly Boy to make them laugh and keep me safe.

Although these two served me well for a number of years, neither Scared Boy or Silly Boy had the right skills to deal with the issues of puberty. So, when I was about 11, my brain looked for other strengths in me that could "save me." It found my sacrificial heart and natural perseverance and formed them into the personality we named Protector. Protector is the one that decided that my sexuality was dangerous and must be hidden "for the good of all" and that it was my lot in life to sacrifice for others and be a victim.

At age 16, when we moved across the country into unfamiliar territory, Angry Boy came to the rescue. The part of me that God intended to fight injustice, set good boundaries, and alert me when those boundaries had been violated, suddenly rose to protect me from the profound loss and abandonment I was feeling at the time. When Angry Boy was in control nothing was more important than getting others before they got me and getting vengeance for those who make me feel like a victim. At that point in my life I seemed angry about anything and everything, but it was that anger that effectively kept people from getting close enough to hurt me.

None of my survival personalities were equipped to deal with the turmoil I felt at age 22 when I was faced with a love relationship and having sex with a real woman for the first time. Although I was scared, Scared Boy's hunkering down tactics wouldn't work well enough in this situation, nor would the humor of Silly Boy, the sacrifices of Protector, or the fury of Angry Boy. A new survival personality had to be developed to deal with new false beliefs that included "if I don't perform sexually, my wife will reject me", "if I let anyone see my true sexuality they will repulsed by me"; and "If I'm not hyper-vigilant in reading a woman's intentions and desires, I'll get hurt." My brain decided that my ability to focus and pay attention to task would be the ideal "savior" for these circumstances—hence Robot was "born."

Through my years of therapy, as my false beliefs were challenged and healed, many of these parts had been restored to their original purpose—they were no longer required to keep me safe. By the time Janet and I got married, Scared Boy, Silly Boy, Protector and Angry Boy only resurfaced in the rarest of situations. Most of the time I was able to let God be my protector instead of relying on these self-made solutions. The last hold out, was Robot. Since many of my earliest and most intense false beliefs equated sexual and gender issues with rejection, I still found it almost impossible to trust God in sexual matters. I continued to rely heavily on my own means of fortifying the walls that kept people from getting too close to me in this vulnerable area.

The Robot was the part that kept me disconnected from both of my wives during sex. They described me as "not being present" or "being on auto-pilot" when we made love. It was a state that was totally fueled by fantasies and was pretty much just "going through the motions" to "satisfy" my woman. Except it wasn't satisfying. Not for them or for me. They just wanted to be seen and loved and all I was able to give them was the physical part of me devoid of emotion or attachment. I WASN'T really there . . . and I didn't know until later, that I was cheating myself out of the best part of physical intimacy, as well.

The first chink in Robot's thick armor came when we did a "Breaking One Flesh Unions" ministry time in Change of Heart. We had first become aware of the spiritual truth of sexual partners becoming "one flesh[19]" in Living Waters. Since then science has confirmed that when a couple is sexually aroused to each other, oxytocin is produced. This hormone creates an invisible bond with anyone you are sexual with. In a marriage oxytocin is a wonderful thing. It makes the couple want to remain close to each other and be intimately associated and bonded. Outside of marriage, however, that bonding and ripping apart of relationships causes us to be fragmented.

God is the only one capable of breaking that one-flesh bond and restoring us to wholeness.

Years before when I was first introduced to the concept, I had asked God to break the one flesh unions created with my ex-wife and the prostitutes I had been with so, as the other people in this current group were preparing a list of people they had been sexual with, I just sat quietly. I was surprised when I felt like God was telling me to write "all the images I have from pornography and fantasies" on my piece of paper. I wondered whether that was OK . . . we'd never talked about such a thing . . . but since it seemed like God was telling me to do it, I did. As the others in the group asked God to break their bond with the names on their papers, I did the same.

I didn't think much more about it until a few nights later, when Janet and I started getting a little amorous. At first we were just cuddling and kissing. I've never had any problem being present during those times—I like cuddling and kissing. But at the point where I would usually reach for a fantasy to go the rest of the way, there was nothing. I tried and tried, but I couldn't come up with a single image. My mind was blank. The fantasies were gone. Robot was out of fuel.

It was the strangest most panicky feeling. I didn't know how to go on, and we didn't that night, but it was the start of us becoming more open sexually. Without my unhealthy tools, I didn't know what to do, so we had to explore it together. It was a good thing, but a very scary thing. I thank God that Janet was patient and made it safe for me to have false starts and panic attacks. It took a long time, but without the fantasies, the Robot was little help and eventually he stopped having a place in our sex life. It wasn't the end to all our problems, but it was a huge step forward.

The serendipitous discovery was that as I learned to join my emotions and even my spirituality with the physical actions of sex, I began to have a whole new experience. The good feelings were intensified and instead of feeling empty and yucky afterwards, I felt the satisfaction and contentment that I had heard others talk about.

Janet . . .

There are a staggering number of marriages in our country in which sex is nonexistent or, at best, highly infrequent for ten, twenty, thirty years or more. Even though many Christians see the sexual addict that turns anorexic as victorious because they are no longer participating in immoral or "sinful" activities, sexual anorexia is not the cure for sexual addiction.

Whether the pendulum swings toward sexual addiction at one end of the spectrum, or sexual anorexia at the other end, it is still an unhealthy relationship with sex and will keep both the individual and their spouse from experiencing the true intimacy that God intended them to have in their marriage.

As we have mentioned numerous times, recovery is usually a slow and often grueling process. It takes courage and stamina to work through all the years of false beliefs and mistrust. Every now and then you slog through periods of cluelessness and frustration. Sometimes it feels like you are the only person in the world that is this messed up, or that you're the only one that doesn't "get it", whatever "it" is. You wonder how God could still love you . . .. or even if He does. It is HARD.

Often we forget that it can be a grueling process for the spouse as well. Not only do their own needs and desires have to be put on the back burner to allow their husband time to heal, but they often experience nagging doubts about their own worth and acceptability as a woman. Will I ever be "enough" for my husband? Is there any hope of ever having the intimate relationship I long for? Will there ever be an end to the slips and the heartbreak that follows? How can I encourage without nagging? Am I being stupid or naïve to even continue in this relationship? There are so many questions without answers. It, too, is HARD.

We long for the healing process to be quick and easy. We want the sanctification process to be as instantaneous as salvation. We so want all our brokenness and fear to just melt away when we first cry out to God and acknowledge His son, Jesus, but, for most of us, recovery means learning how to work together with God to become the person He always meant us to be.

It is similar to going to a new doctor that you've been told is an expert in treating physical problems like the one you have been experiencing. It is not merely meeting the doctor that heals you, it is the process he takes you through that brings you back to health. Much of that process involves his capable diagnosis and knowledge of appropriate treatment, but sometimes there are things that we must do, under his guidance, to aid in the recovery.

The Great Physician also knows what is required for our complete healing and freedom from those things that torment us. Although He has every ability to heal us instantly, He often asks us to go through a process to get to that place of healing.

God wants an intimate relationship with us. He knows that it is our weaknesses that force us to turn to him and it is in that turning that we learn to trust Him and let His divine strength replace our human frailties. He often allows some of our struggles to remain for a season to help direct us to Him and His sovereign power. It is through the recovery process that we really begin to know our Creator and our God in an intimate way and learn how to allow His abundant grace to be sufficient to meet our needs and fill our empty spots.

Whether you are the one looking for recovery from addiction, or the spouse grappling with questions about her own self-worth and feelings of rejection, your struggle has nothing to do with whether you love God enough or have enough faith. It only says that you still have a ways to go in honing your ability and willingness to risk trusting God with your fears. You're not alone—we all do! As imperfect humans, none of us have yet learned to fully trust God in ALL things. Every one of us is still a work in progress!

27

As For Me . . .
I Choose Life!

Leaving the Addiction Behind and Finding Real Freedom

Bruce . . .

For the first time in my life, I truly know that people who have struggled with sexual addiction, like me, can find a TOTAL healing. For a long time I believed that although I could get a lot of healing, the addiction would always be sitting on my shoulder waiting for the opportunity to bring me down. I was convinced that there would always be periodic slips and their consequences to contend with.

Today I can say I am enjoying a freedom that only God can give. I know that it is not just that I am trying harder to "do better"—my heart has actually changed from the inside out. I first noticed it soon after I found out that one of the adult video stores I used to frequent was going out of business. The newspaper article said the closing wasn't because there was no longer a demand for pornography, but because the owner felt he couldn't compete with the ease and convenience of accessing pornography on the Internet. Anyway, a few days later, I was heading out to do some errands and the thought crossed my mind that I should stop by their big clearance sale "for old times sake." But, just as quickly as the thought came in, my mind countered it with, "Nah, I like where I am, now. I don't want to go back to that anymore." And, without another thought, I didn't!

I don't want to come off as too overconfident. I DO know the fast track for getting back there. The four most dangerous things in our lives are self-reliance, resentment, stress, and deprivation. Any one of them, left unchecked, will lead to a dangerous sense of entitlement. No matter what excessive behavior we are trying to avoid—eating, spending, drinking, drugging, sex, or any number of other things, letting ourselves get to a place where we feel entitled to a "reward" because of our struggles or accomplishments, puts us in imminent danger of a relapse.

Acknowledging and resolving the issues that come up in our lives is the best insurance against the grip of entitlement. Resentment, depression, victim thinking and stress all come from our inability to admit and do something about what we're feeling. As I have learned to let myself feel anger and stress, I have been able to talk and pray about them and find ways to deal with them. Once an issue has been resolved it goes away. I don't have to mull it over, and let it fester until I become resentful or depressed. I am free of it.

I realize now, that I DO have choices—not about the hand I am dealt in life, but about what I do with it. I am only a victim when I CHOOSE not to play any cards. When I quit the game, there is no hope of winning. God told me to choose between life or death. He didn't say "you got a bad deal and you have to live with it." I can choose to be a victim. I can choose to act on every impulse, like a child, or I can choose to grow up and reach out to those who can help me.

Self-reliance and isolation go hand in hand for me. Every time I've caught myself saying "I can handle this without telling anyone" I've known I was in trouble. Even though it is often scary, we need God and other people. Because of shame and pride it took me a long time to realize how essential it was to let other people into my life. Today I am surrounded by safe people who aren't threatened or traumatized when I admit my weaknesses and struggles. They don't have to fix me or give me advice. They just love and support me as a person. In addition to friends and family, I have sought out men, some in recovery and others that are not, to befriend. Openly sharing my testimony has provided me with a myriad of people who, just by knowing my story, provide me with a form of accountability, and continuing to work with people that are new to recovery helps remind me of where I've been and why I don't want to be there again.

Any time we vow never to do something, we set ourselves up for doing the very thing we are depriving ourselves of. Instead of focusing on what I don't want to do, I have turned to look at where I DO want to go. I am seeking the things that make me feel healthy and strong and free. It is the push and pull of recovery. Our journey begins when the consequences of our actions push us into recovery, but in time, we find that we have turned a corner and are being pulled forward by the good that comes out of making different choices. At that point we are no longer enslaved by the addiction. We can live without the fear and paranoia that we may fail at any moment.

I'm far from "finished." I regularly run into areas of my life that still need God's touch. I'm still just a sinner saved by grace. I'm not perfect. I periodically have days when I forget that I have choices and I don't have to be a victim. I'm still a little sensitive about the possibility of being rejected. I still have troubles initiating sex at times . . . and I'm often so busy trying to "read" what Janet wants in our most intimate moments that I don't take the time to explore what I want, need, and feel but, in spite of all that, I am in awe at just how far God has brought me out of the grip of death.

I am experiencing things now, that I never dreamed I would or could have when I was still active in my addiction:

- *I am physically healthier than I've been in years. I'm not sick nearly as often as I was when I was acting out and in early recovery.*

- *I am not depressed anymore. I was able to go off the anti-depressants I had taken for years and I'm still*

> OK. I struggle with the regular ups and downs of life, but I'm not stuck in that deep hole I lived in so long.

- *I am able to feel more connected to my wife and the other people around me. I don't feel alienated and alone anymore.*

- *I am coming to understand that I don't have to be a victim. I am realizing that there are things I can do and say that can change the effects of what life throws my way.*

- *I'm actually living life now—I'm not just existing or surviving.*

- *I can feel. Sometimes they're good feelings, sometimes they're not, but I'm grateful that I'm not trapped in that awful numbness anymore.*

- *I don't sexualize women the way I used to. I see them as valuable, interesting people and not just objects.*

- *I can accept the fact that women have a sexuality, too—they're not only there to accept a man's sexuality. Sex is not just "done" to them, it can be reciprocal.*

- *I feel comfortable and at peace about platonic relationships between men and women. In spite of what my mother told me, it's OK to be friends with girls.*

- *I feel safe around God. I don't feel like he's waiting to get me.*

- *I am at peace with the idea that I can have different emotions toward God. I don't have to pretend to be something I'm not. I'm not always OK, but I'm OK with giving God my "not OK."*

- *I've come to terms with the fact that I am not all good or all bad. I can give my whole self to God without trying to hide the bad parts.*

- *I no longer believe that I am uniquely sinful. God told me that I'm no worse or no better than other sinners. I know that I am forgiven.*

- *I have come to know God and His character better. I realize that he sees me differently than I see myself.*

- *I also realize that I am much more than a sex addict. I have noteworthy talents and strengths. Sex no longer consumes 98% of my waking hours, it has become one small and enjoyable part of my life.*

All the time and effort I've put into recovery work, no matter how difficult, pales in comparison to the things I've gained. There is a way that leads to life and not to death. That's the one I want to stay on.

Janet . . .

Over the years, Bruce has willingly added safeguards to his life, to help him during his weak times. Although I refuse to take the role of "warden", I now balance both of our separate bank accounts each month (partly because Bruce doesn't really like doing it, and partly because just knowing that I will see his expenditures has been a bit of a deterrent during times of temptation.) Since he knows that in the past his secrets have caused us both pain, he increasingly makes a point of talking about his feelings and fears, plans and whereabouts. His concern for how his actions have and do affect me and his willingness to share so vulnerably causes me to respect him more than ever before.

God has shown Bruce and I the importance of love and respect in a marriage even in the face of difficult challenges like addiction. An often quoted verse in Ephesians 5:33 instructs us that a man must love his wife as he loves himself and the wife must respect her husband. We've probably all heard sermons and marriage seminars on how a husband should love his wife unconditionally, but much less has been said about respecting a husband who is involved in unrespectable behaviors.

The core emotional need of a man is. . .surprise, surprise . . . respect. More than anything a man wants. . .no, NEEDS. . to feel respected. Almost every wife I have ever counseled, has countered that thought with "but how can I respect him when he is doing such detestable things? Doesn't respect have to be earned? Someone doing what he's doing doesn't deserve respect." But, the Bible doesn't say "a wife should respect her husband if he has earned it," it says "a wife must respect her husband." She MUST, because her relationship will never be what God intended if she doesn't . . . in fact it may not survive at all.

What a man yearns to hear from his wife is "I believe in you," "You may not be doing everything right, but I believe you have what it takes to get past this," "Even though you are struggling and failing, you are more than an addict .You have other good qualities and they and your relationship with God will help you get through this." This kind of unconditional respect says "I believe you can do this."

It doesn't say, "well, that's how all guys are" . . . that's the best you can expect from them . . . they don't know how to be faithful . . . they don't know how to keep their pants zipped . . .they're just insensitive and selfish. It is demeaning and disrespectful to think that someone is incapable of growing and changing and persevering to freedom. Almost without exception we have found the sex addicts we have worked with are caring, sensitive men, hiding behind a wall of pain and self-destruction.

As For Me . . . I Choose Life!

I can't say that I have always hit the mark when it comes to showing respect to Bruce. Sometimes I have been too pushy. Sometimes, in my own hurt and anger, I have said unkind things. Sometimes when I have been scared I have had to go to God and have him remind me why I can believe in Bruce. At times I have had to apologize to my husband and reaffirm that I DO believe in him. And that belief has sometimes helped him keep going when he has had a hard time believing in himself. Together we are stronger than he could be alone. I cannot do his recovery for him, but I can encourage him in HIS efforts.

I can't guarantee that Bruce will never make wrong choices again, but I am encouraged by his perseverance and his desire for a complete recovery. He is working hard to pay attention to the times he starts to isolate or feel like a victim. He is learning to talk about the things that are bugging him and not just accept bad things as his due in life.

For the first time since he was a young boy, he says he feels completely free. As he puts it, "The addiction is no longer sitting on my shoulder looking for an opportunity."

Even though I've only walked part of Bruce's recovery journey with him, it has definitely had some rocky patches. There have been days when I really wondered if God knew what he was doing when he chose me for this adventure, but there have been an even greater number of days when I have felt blessed and honored to be a tool in God's hand and a witness to not only my husband's healing, but to the recovery quest of some of the most courageous men I've ever met.

Bruce asked me just the other day . . . "If you had known then, what you know now, would you have married me?"

The answer is a resounding "yes."

Epilogue

Message from Bruce

If you picked up this book there is a good chance that you, or someone you love, struggles with the same problem that plagued me for nearly 40 years. There was a time that I was in exactly the same place you are now. I was thinking and feeling the same things you are today.

Initially, one of my biggest concerns about letting my story be written was that it is virtually impossible for the retelling of someone's story to realistically convey the time, pain and complexities of facing this issue. Although I think my wife has done an excellent job of capturing the pain and struggle I experienced, the very nature of a book condenses months and years of struggles and resolves them in mere paragraphs and pages. It makes recovery seem deceptively quick and easy. In real-time, the process is neither quick nor easy, but with the help of God and others it is possible. There is hope!

As much as we wish it weren't so . . . the absolute truth is . . . you can't do recovery alone. This addiction thrives on isolation. You need people to come alongside you. Reaching out is probably the hardest thing anyone will every ask you to do—but it was absolutely essential to my healing and it will be to yours as well.

The idea of talking to someone about our darkest secrets and greatest fears is terrorizing. I remember those feelings well. I used to think that I was a coward because I was so full of fear, but I learned that courageous people have just as many fears as cowards, they just refuse to let them hold them back. They choose to move forward in spite of their fear. The end result is new life, hope and FREEDOM. No matter where you are today, or what you've done—that freedom is available to YOU.

The most difficult thing is that we can't control how others will respond to our struggles. Since I already condemned myself more than anyone else possibly could, I expected condemnation and rejection from everyone around me. And, sometimes, that's what I got. But, just as often, people surprised me. Instead of feeling their revulsion and judgment, I experienced acceptance, empathy and encouragement. It gave me the courage to persevere.

And then— in the midst of all the struggle—I began to learn more about the character of God, as well. Little by little, as I let my walls down, I met a God who, unbelievably, looked beyond the things I did and called out the spirit of life in me.

What God told me is entirely true for you, as well . . .
It's time to choose life.

Endnotes

CHAPTER SEVEN
1. Genesis 2:18
2. *National Health and Social Life Survey* 1994 (Edward O. Laumann, Robert T. Michaels, John H Gagnon & Stuart Michaels) (Chicago: University of Chicago Press, 1994)

CHAPTER ELEVEN
3. Romans 7:15-20
4. In his book, *Don't Call it Love—Recovery from Sexual Addiction,* (Bantam, 1991), Patrick Carnes PhD, reports that as many as 72% of sex addicts have been physically abused; 81% sexually abused and 97% emotionally abused.

CHAPTER THIRTEEN
5. *Out of the Shadows* by Patrick Carnes (a pioneer in the field of sexual addiction), (Minn: CompCare Publishers ,1983)

CHAPTER SIXTEEN
6. Laurens Van der Post, South African writer/philosopher (1906-1996)

CHAPTER SEVENTEEN
7. Eye Movement Desensitization and Reprocessing Therapy

CHAPTER EIGHTEEN
[8] Some of the more helpful books Bruce initially read included:
The Courage to Heal, by Ellen Bass and Laura Davis, (Harper & Row Publishers, Inc., 1988)
Victims No Longer, by Mike Lew (Harper & Row Publishers, Inc. 1988, 1990)
Our Sexual Healing Journey by Wendy Maltz (Harper Collins Publishing, Inc. 1991)

CHAPTER NINETEEN
[9] 1 Peter 3:8-11
[10] Matthew 22:37-39
[11] Romans 12:15-16
[12] Romans 12:4-8
[13] Galatians 6:1-2; James 5:19-20

CHAPTER TWENTY
[14] *I See the Lord,* Andy Park & Mark McCoy ©1995 Mercy/Vineyard Publishing (ASCAP) Admin. in North America by Music Services o/b/o Vineyard Music USA. All Rights Reserved. Used by Permission.
[15] Isaiah 6:3-8

CHAPTER TWENTY-THREE
[16] *Amazed,* From LoneStar's Album *Lonely Grill* ©1999 Warner-Tamerlane Publishing Corp./ Golden Wheat Music (BMI)
[17] *The Five Love Languages: How to Express Heartfelt Commitment to your Mate* by Dr. Gary Chapman (Northfield Press, 1992)
[18] Gary Thomas, author of *Sacred Marriage: What if God Designed Marrriage to Make Us Holy More than to Make Us Happy?* (Zondervan, 2000)

CHAPTER TWENTY-SIX
[19] Matthew 19:4-6 or Mark 10:7-9

To Contact Bruce & Janet

Bruce and Janet are both affiliated with
Life More Abundant Network
Bellingham, Washington
360-223-1862

*For more information about sexual addiction
or Life More Abundant Network please visit our website:*
www.lifemoreabundant.net

For daily encouragement we invite you to read our blog:
blog.lifemoreabundant.net

Contact either of us directly via Janet's e-mail:
janet@lifemoreabundant.net

Made in the USA
San Bernardino, CA
02 April 2013